A
BALANCED
CHURCH

BOOKS BY CHARLES W. CONN

BIBLICAL

The Bible: Book of Books
A Guide to the Pentateuch
Highlights of Hebrew History
Christ and the Gospels
Acts of the Apostles
Survey of the Epistles

DEVOTIONAL

The Rudder and the Rock
A Certain Journey
The Pointed Pen

DOCTRINAL

Pillars of Pentecost
Why Men Go Back
A Balanced Church

HISTORICAL

Like a Mighty Army
Where the Saints Have Trod
The Evangel Reader

CHARLES W. CONN

A BALANCED CHURCH

Introduction by
Ray H. Hughes

PATHWAY PRESS
Cleveland, Tennessee
1975

A BALANCED CHURCH

THIRD PRINTING

Library of Congress Catalog Card Number:
75-8082

Printed in the United States of America

TO FRANKLIN
MY BROTHER

*who is also my brother in Christ
and my colleague in the ministry.*

INTRODUCTION

The Bible says that "of making many books there is no end." But this is not just another book. In my opinion it will prove to be one of the most significant contributions in this generation to the body of evangelical and Pentecostal thought and literature. There has been a proliferation of books on the subject of spiritual gifts during the past decade, some of which have left much to be desired.

Dr. Charles W. Conn has an advantage over many who have undertaken to write on such subjects. He does not speak as an observer or as one who has recently come to the knowledge of *charismata,* but as one who has spent a lifetime researching, teaching and writing on it and kindred subjects. In this book he brings together the material belonging to this great topic with systematizing genius and presents it with a richness of apprehension that is rare. He also knows by personal experience the things of and pertaining to the Spirit, which fact affords him the spiritual insight necessary to deal with such profound areas of thought. He discusses in a singularly profound manner the depth of the operation of the Holy Spirit in the life of a believer.

In this treatise the writes addresses himself to some of the problem areas and proceeds to give direction to the church. For example, he deals with the relationship of the Gifts of the Spirit to the Fruit of the Spirit. Contrary to the teaching of some Bible scholars, Dr. Conn propounds that "the Gifts of the Spirit cannot work independently of the Fruit of the Spirit. Since both are manifestations of the same Spirit, they will at all times be in agreement with, and will complement, one another. It is error to imagine that one can bypass the Fruit and receive the Gifts. No one can leapfrog over the Fruit of the Spirit into the realm of the Gifts of the Spirit. Any apparent manifestation of the Gifts without the Fruit is exactly that—an appearance, not reality." Thus the writer places the Fruit of the Spirit in its proper perspective—a prerequisite to the operation of the Gifts.

The Trinity is possibly the most difficult theological doctrine to understand. Yet the writer in an illustrative manner sets forth this truth concisely and in understandable terms develops a high level of theological clarity.

This volume also points up that the balance of Christian living centers in Christlikeness. It strikes a balance of the negative and positive elements of Christian living. The openminded reader will doubtlessly conclude that both the Fruit and Gifts are necessary for a balanced church. They are not luxuries for the spiritual aristocracy but essentials for balanced Christian service.

I have been fortunate through the years to have had the privilege of hearing most of the contents of this study in lecture form, by which throngs of people have been inspired, enlightened and brought to maturity in Christ. I therefore have firsthand knowledge of the effect that this book will have on its readers.

I commend it to all levels of the ministry, for the work of the ministry and for the perfecting of the saints. It should be taught in all churches, recommended to new converts, and to those who want to be introduced to a life in the Spirit. Certainly no one will ever peruse these pages without perceiving that it is a very valuable gift from the treasure chest of a Bible teacher of renown and a writer *par excellence*. I earnestly commend this volume to the attention of all who would know more about the fullness of the Spirit as a stimulating and an enlightening study.

A treatise of this type is very rare. True to its title, it is a balanced work.

Ray H. Hughes, Ed.D., Litt.D.
Chairman
Pentecostal Fellowship of
North America

FOREWORD

This book has been thirty-five years in the making. For that period of time I have been consistently and heartily involved in the study of the Scriptures, especially as they relate to God's instructions to modern man.

In the Scriptures it is clear that Christ expects His followers to be the extension of His ministry on earth. To enable man for such a gigantic task, He sent the Holy Spirit into the world to identify, empower and guide all who receive Him.

The Pentecostal movement of this century began at a time when the religious world was in a state of apathy and growing unbelief. The outpouring of the Holy Spirit was like a breath of fresh air that blew away the gathering mists of modernism and secularism. I happily became a part of the Pentecostal movement and have witnessed its development through two-thirds of my lifetime. During the early days of the revival, the Pentecostal message was called the Full Gospel. It was believed that the movement restored the fullness of the gospel that had been embraced by the apostles but had been lost in subsequent centuries. Its return and recovery heralded a "latter rain."

The Full Gospel is not liturgical, sacerdotal or formal. It is simple belief in the Scriptures, accepting of spiritual fullness, and enthusiasm in worship. The Scriptures are accepted as the full and inerrant Word of God, a belief that stands unshaken in this day. Distinctives of the movement are the practice of holy living, simplicity of worship and expectancy of Christ to be in the midst of His church.

It is my prayer that this study will contribute to an understanding of the Full Gospel message and articulate it in a way that can be comprehended and understood by men of this time. I have given the substance of the book as a series of lectures in many parts of the world, and to numerous denominations of the Pentecostal movement. I pray that the message will be received in printed form with the same attention it has been received from the speaker's platform.

****

A number of persons assisted me in bringing this study to the printed page. First, I appreciate the thousands who have attended the lectures in Bible conferences, conventions, Bible institutes and colleges around the world. Their eagerness to hear the Word of God has been inspiring and highly motivating.

My long-time secretary, Mrs. Evaline Echols, transcribed and copy-edited the manuscript from my handwritten copy, oral dictation and recorded lectures. She is largely responsible for the indices that follow the text. Ron Hood has illustrated the work with line drawings and Lonzo Kirkland has captured the theme of the book with his cover design. I am grateful for their assistance. Dr. Ray H. Hughes has introduced the study with his astute observations.

I especially appreciate those personal friends and colleagues who took time to read the text and offer helpful comments: Dr. Percy S. Brewster, Dr. Howard Courtney, Dr. Wade H. Horton, Dr. Ray Smith, Dr. Robert Taitinger, Dr. J. Floyd Williams and Dr. Thomas F. Zimmerman. Their comments appear at the end of the book.

My faithful wife Edna should share in the completed work as she has shared in the ministry that produced it. She is a living example of every grace and virtue mentioned in this book.

Charles W. Conn, Litt.D.

Lee College
Cleveland, Tennessee
May, 1975

CONTENTS

PART ONE

THE TRINITY AND THE CHURCH

And Simon Peter answered and said, Thou art the Christ, the Son of the living God. And Jesus answered and said unto him, Blessed art thou, Simon Barjona: for flesh and blood hath not revealed it unto thee, but my Father which is in heaven (Matthew 16:16, 17).

Go ye therefore, and teach all nations, baptizing them in the name of the Father, and of the Son, and of the Holy Ghost: Teaching them to observe all things whatsoever I have commanded you: and, lo, I am with you alway, even unto the end of the world. Amen (Matthew 28: 19, 20).

1
THE TRINITY AND THE CHURCH

PROLOGUE

Jesus led His eleven companions up the gentle slope of the Mount of Olives, the loose rocks along the path stirring and crunching under their sandaled feet. Across the yawning ravine below them, the distant, busy sounds of Jerusalem grew faint, then faded away altogether.

From the crest of the historic mountain Jesus could see the ancient walled city, its lights blinking on as it settled down for the night. All along its twisting, narrow streets merchants closed their shops and put away their wares. Vendors shut their stalls and made their weary way home through the darkened, odor-filled streets. As mothers called their children in from play, childish laughter blended with the subdued sounds of evening.

In the great Temple that dominated the city, evening prayers and ritual were made by the solemn priests. Except for the few who had accepted Jesus as the Messiah, life in Jerusalem went on as usual.

On the rocky Olivet crest, which sloped gently eastward to Bethany, one of the most extraordinary events of all time was about to take place. Jesus was ready to commit His earthly ministry into the hands of His followers and return to His place in heaven.

His face resplendent with the light that comes with understanding and confidence, Jesus spoke to His waiting, questioning apostles. Eleven of them were there; Judas was dead and must be replaced. As the stars winked on in the heavens, Jesus said, "Stay in Jerusalem until the promise of the Father comes upon you. You shall be baptized with the Holy Ghost within a few days."

The disciples asked Him, "Lord, will you at this time restore the kingdom to Israel?"

Jesus assured them that such was not His intention. He had no civil authority to give them. They would, however, receive spiritual power after the Holy Ghost came upon them. In this power of the Spirit, "Ye shall be witnesses unto me both in Jerusalem, and in all Judaea, and in Samaria, and unto the uttermost part of the earth."

Having spoken, Jesus lifted His hands and blessed His followers; then, before their very eyes, He moved majestically into heaven. He quickly disappeared in the soft embrace of a cloud and was not seen again.

Robbed of His presence, the night was startlingly still and lonely and quiet. The eleven apostles were suddenly alone. Their aloneness was intensified by their sense that the task of Jesus was now their task. In the womb of silence the disciples became aware of two persons, radiant and white, standing among them. The men were messengers of God, who said: "Jesus will come again in the same manner that He has disappeared."

In awe the disciples then filed down the side of the

mountain. The muted sounds of Jerusalem grew loud again as they neared the city where they would wait for the promise of the Father. They were thrust back into the noisy, needy world which they must reach with the gospel of their departed Lord.

His followers were all that Jesus left. They were the foundation of the church, the continuation of His life. In a very real sense they would continue the ministry He had begun. He left them no treasury, no land, no property, no status. But He left them much, very much, with which to do the work committed unto them. And that which He gave them would prove adequate for their task. Ten days later they were filled with the Holy Spirit and their labor began.

THE BODY OF CHRIST

When Christ returned to heaven following His crucifixion and resurrection He commissioned His followers to continue and complete His earthly work. He left them to do what He would have done if His life had not been cut short; during the brief span of His life He had laid the foundation upon which His disciples were to build. This commission to carry on His work has not changed, but remains the responsibility of the church today.

Since Christ's work consisted of what He *was,* what He *said,* and what He *did,* we have a responsibility to be (1) a continuation of His life, (2) an amplification of His message, and (3) an extension of His works.

Simply stated, the mission of the church of Jesus Christ is to do in our day what He would do if He were personally on the earth. This is an extraordinary assignment and calls for extraordinary powers. Human strength will not suffice to do the work of the church, so we must have spiritual provision and resources if we are to represent Him adequately.

The wonderful thing is that Jesus did not leave the church
without the necessary resources, but He gave it all the elements required to function as He would do. In Him we
are able to *be* what we ought to be, *say* what we ought to
say, and *do* what we ought to do.

In Scripture the church is always represented as being an
extension of Christ. He used two metaphors to emphasize
this relationship. In one, which He used on the evening
before His crucifixion, He called Himself the Vine, with
His followers extending from Him as branches (John 15:
1-8). Paul in his epistles called the church "the body of
Christ," of which Christ is the head (1 Corinthians 12:
27; Colossians 1:18). In these relationships we are united
with Christ as a body is united with its head, and as a
branch is united with its vine. This relationship requires
that we be of His spirit, His nature, His essence and His
purpose. Just as the head cannot be of one kind and the
body another, so we must be *of* Him, *in* Him and *like*
Him. It is a biological impossibility for a vine to be of
one species and the branches another. Whatever the vine
is the branches will be also; the kind of fruit borne by
the branches is determined by the nature of the vine. And
this fact is even more conspicuous with a head and a body.
The head cannot be of one species and the body of another—what the one is the other must be also. Disparity of
species is as spiritually impossible as it would be biologically
monstrous.

Implicit in these metaphoric examples is the truth that we
must be in our generation what He would be if He were
on earth today. We must have the spiritual coordination and
force, the religious form and symmetry and the moral
strength and perfection that is appropriate to Him. Only
when we possess these qualities can we truly be His
Church.

THE HOLY SPIRIT

When Christ committed His mission and ministry to His followers, He promised to send them the Holy Spirit to serve as their guide, to instruct and empower them (John 14:12-18; 16:13). Through the Holy Spirit we have all the spiritual equipment and provision we require to be what we should and to do what we must. It is in the Holy Ghost, and by the Holy Ghost in us, that Christ Himself is still in the world today (John 14:18). It is in the Holy Ghost that we are empowered and equipped to function as the body of Christ and bear fruit as the branch of the Vine.

While Jesus was on earth He was limited to being in one place at one time, and His life was bound by the measure of His years. But the Holy Ghost is not restricted by space or time—the Spirit is in all the earth forever. He manifests His power and performs His purpose wherever there is a yielded and believing heart.

There is nothing haphazard or accidental about what the church is to be or do. In establishing His church the Lord left nothing to chance. He has given us all the elements and qualities that befit us as His representatives. As we shall see later, there are three elements or components with which the church is endowed.

THE TRINITY

In Scripture all numbers have a special significance, a fact that, though not invariable, we find important to our study. The number "one," for example, is the number of unity and primacy; "two" is the number of unity and fellowship, and conversely of division and separation; and "three" is the number of completeness and perfection. The number seven also represents perfection and completeness in God's work. The importance of the seventh day, the Sabbath, illustrates the importance of the number in the Judeo-Christian faith. All other numbers similarly have their special significance, but these suffice as examples at this time.

As we shall now discover, the number "three" has a special significance for the church. We first encounter the number three in the revelation of God, for there is one God in three persons—the Father, Son, and Holy Ghost (Matthew 28:19). This revelation of the Trinity—the Triune God—is basic to all spiritual understanding. There is an old medieval design, the earliest graphic representation of the Trinity, that shows each member of the Trinity to be a complete entity, and yet shows how none is truly complete without the other two.

The original Latin language used in this Trinitarian design was in keeping with the ecclesiastical usage of ancient times. Pater means "Father"; Filius means "Son"; Spiritus Sanctimus means "Holy Spirit"; and Deus means "God."

The Father is not the Son, but He is God; the Son is not the Holy Spirit, but He is God; the Holy Spirit is not the Father, but He is God. Each of the three is fully God, but neither is all there is of God. Now let us change this design into English and we will see the modern truth of this old representation.

For the purposes of our study, we will now simplify the ancient design into a triangle. A triangle is a clear example of how three are required to make one, with three equal angles, each united with the other two, forming a triad of balance and strength. The primary angle of the triangle must represent the Father for He is first of all in the Godhead, but observe that the Father alone does not constitute all there is of God.

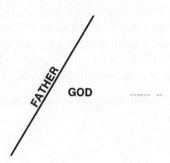

If the Father were all there is of God, He would be complete, just as the single angle is complete. But the whole would be different from what it is—it would not be in accordance with the revelation of the Godhead as we understand it from the Scriptures.

While the Father is primary in the Godhead, and all Divinity proceeds from Him, He is united with the Son: so we draw another line, equal to the Father, and this represents the Son, "Who, being in the form of God, thought it not robbery to be equal with God" (Philippians 2:6).

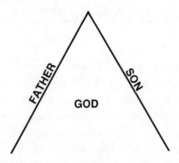

But the Father and the Son do not constitute the fullness of God; the Holy Spirit is also God and He is required for Divine completeness. This perfection is seen in the completed pattern of the Trinity, and in the completed pattern there is strength, beauty, harmony, and purpose without end.

Now our image of God is complete. The Father, Son, and
Holy Ghost are not three Gods: they are a Tri-unity, three
personalities who constitute one identity of God. Each is
complete in Himself, yet together the Three form a higher
completeness. They Three are One, and without any one the
Godhead would be incomplete. Each joins, and is joined
by; supports, and is supported by, the other two. The Father
exists in unity with the Son and the Holy Spirit; the Son
exists in unity with the Father and the Holy Spirit; and the
Holy Spirit exists in unity with the Father and the Son. Each
of the three exists in unity with the other two as equal parts
to one whole. Each is necessary to, and dependent upon, the
other two; and while each is individually perfect, the three
are required for completeness, perfection and balance.

Although the word "Trinity" is not found in Scripture, its
truth is everywhere indicated or revealed. The revelation of
the Trinity began in the Old Testament with the plural
declaration of One God (Genesis 1:26; 3:22; 11:7; Isaiah
6:8), and was completed in the New Testament when the
Son was revealed by incarnation and the Holy Spirit was
revealed by infilling. Several scriptures clearly declare the
existence of the Triune God: "For there are three that bear
record in heaven, the Father, the Word, and the Holy Ghost:
and these three are one," (1 John 5:7). Also, "Go ye
therefore, and teach all nations, baptizing them in the name
of the Father, and of the Son, and of the Holy Ghost"
(Matthew 28:19), and "The grace of the Lord Jesus Christ,
and the love of God, and the communion of the Holy Ghost,
be with you all. Amen" (2 Corinthians 13:14). Other scriptures strongly intimate the Trinity with reference to the
Father, Son, and Holy Spirit (Mark 1:10, 11; John 14:16;
1 Corinthians 12:4-6). The Father is not the Son and the
Son is not the Holy Spirit, but the Father is God, the Son
is God, the Holy Spirit is God. No one of the three is the

entirety of God, but each is all God. God is the Three together in unity. This is a Divine mystery, a truth to be
spiritually accepted but not always comprehended by the
human intellect.

A. H. Strong, a distinguished theologian of the last generation, spoke of the mystery of the Trinity in this way:

> In the nature of the one God there are three eternal
> distinctions which are represented to us under the figure
> of persons, and these three are equal. This tripersonality
> of the Godhead is exclusively a truth of revelation. It is
> clearly, though not formally, made known in the New Tes-
> tament, and intimations of it may be found in the Old.[1]

A contemporary theologian, the late Lewis Sperry Chafer,
mentioned the intellectual difficulty of the doctrine:

> The fact that there are three Persons in One is a revela-
> tion which belongs to the sphere of Heaven's perfect under-
> standing (1 Corinthians 13:12), and while we can now be-
> lieve and receive all that God has said to us, these truths
> cannot be compressed into the limited sphere of human
> understanding. There is one God who subsists in a three-
> fold personality. The Father says "I," the Son says "I," and
> the Spirit, also, is in every sense a person; yet these Three
> are not three Persons, but they are One. They are equal,
> and to them should be ascribed the same attributes, titles,
> adoration, worship, and confidence; yet they are not three
> Gods, but they are one God. In this divine relationship,
> three Persons are seen to be One; yet without blending or
> confounding the separateness of their infinite Beings. And
> in like manner, One Person is seen to be Three without a
> dividing of substance. The Trinity consists in three essential
> distinctions in the substance of the one God; yet these dis-
> tinctions are presented as separate persons to the extent that
> the Father sends the Son into the world (John 17:18),
> and the Son sends the Spirit into the world (John 16:7). This
> procession or exercise of authority, it should be observed, is
> never reversed. If all this seems incomprehensible, it is only
> because the finite mind is unable to grasp infinite truth.[2]

MAN—THE IMAGE OF GOD

When God created man it was in His own image. Having already created the beasts of the field, the birds of the air, and the fish of the sea; He then created man, the highest order of creation, the only creature capable of communion with the Creator. If man had been created with body alone he would have been like a beast, earthbound, incapable of Divine communication and fellowship. So we draw a horizontal line to represent this visible, material earthbound quality of man:

BODY

But God made man infinitely higher than all other earthly creatures. He inclined man upward and gave him a heavenward capacity. In simple terms God endowed man with much of Himself. In Genesis 1:26, God said, "Let *us* make man in *our* image, after *our* likeness. . . ." Note that He said *our* image, not *my* image. What is "our likeness"? It is the likeness of the Three, which we have already noted to be best represented by a triad of equal and united parts. The form of man in 1 Thessalonians 5:23 is also three: spirit, soul and body. In the three parts there is unity and harmony. Neither part constitutes the whole of man any more than one person of the Godhead is all of God. Man follows the image of God by being one person of three parts.

Some men use Genesis 1:26 in an effort to prove that God and man are alike in physical appearance, but the meaning is infinitely greater than that. It means that we are created in the likeness of the Godhead, the Trinity—Father, Son and

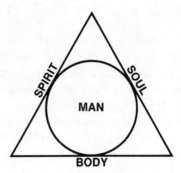

Holy Spirit. In their image we have spirit, soul and body, neither of which alone would make us a man, but which together do. We will place the two together and see how man is indeed in the image of God, and this symbol will for our further purposes represent both God and man.

As we shall see, man was made to be like God. Not in the perverted sense of being a god, as Satan tempted Adam and Eve in the Garden of Eden, but like Him in completeness and holiness of life and purpose. Man alone of all God's earthly creatures is capable of having fellowship and communion with his Creator.

There are scriptural references to the relationship triune man has with the Triune God. For example, the spirit of man is called the candle of Jehovah, the Father (Proverbs 20:27); Jesus, the Son, is the Shepherd and Bishop of man's soul (1 Peter 2:25); and the body of man is the "temple of the Holy Ghost" (1 Corinthians 6:19). While there is spiritual significance in these associations, we shall not dwell on them in this study. I point them out merely to indicate the marvelous manner in which man is created in the image of the Trinity.

God created man in His image in order that the Creator might have fellowship with the creature. To further the possibility of this fellowship, He gave man three of His Divine attributes:

WILL

CONSCIENCE

ETERNITY

Will is given to man so he can by dedication and devotion lift himself to be a son of God. Contrariwise, by degeneracy and sin man can also reduce himself to be a child of the devil. Free will makes this self-determination possible for man, but a beast can only follow the course of instinct and nature. Man does not serve God out of compulsion, but desire, while beasts follow nature and instinct without choice or decision. When a lion sees a deer he does not make a moral choice as to whether or not he should slay the deer. If he is hungry he kills and devours the deer without a thought. I have heard that there are certain birds that will not intermate, but remain with one mate for an entire mating season or for life. The birds are not to be commended for this chastity, for it comes about by creature instinct instead

of by will and decision. It is divinely different with a man,
for he is given will by which he comes to his goodness or
sinks to his evil.

Conscience is given to man in order that he may reflect on
his ways and order his life. No beast reflects upon his brute
behavior with regret, he simply follows his nature without
question or contemplation. He has no pangs of remorse and
makes no resolves for correction. But man can order his steps
aright; he can correct his course when it is wrong and amend
his base nature by surrendering it to God. Conscience causes
a man to look within himself, and this introspection leads
to an improvement of his life—or it reduces him to sinful
hardness.

Eternity is synonymous with God, for only He is sufficient
to occupy eternity, and only eternity is vast enough to con-
tain God. Yet God has shared even this attribute with man
so that he shall live forever. When a beast dies he is dead
forever, but when a man dies he shall live again. We are
more than flesh—we are also spirit and soul. Being such,
we shall never die and our fellowship with the Lord shall
be eternal. We are meant for communion with God, and
no man can rest until he has discovered this Divine fellowship. God has endowed us with much of Himself and we
are imperfect until we establish harmony with Him.

THE THREEFOLD FELLOWSHIP

Following the pattern He used for Himself and man, God
has established the church as an institution of three elements.
This perfect pattern is seen in all aspects of God's relationship with man.

The Tabernacle. The Tabernacle, which was the earliest
form of the church, consisted of three individual parts: the
Court, the Holy Place and the Holy of Holies. Each of the

three sections did the service of God and was necessary to the Tabernacle. The absence of either section would have made it incomplete.

Moral Requirement. Also in the Old Testament, God established a threefold requirement for man's righteousness: "He hath shewed thee, O man, what is good; and what doth the Lord require of thee, but to do justly, and to love mercy, and to walk humbly with thy God?" (Micah 6:8). This requirement, like the Mosaic economy, is insufficient for New Testament living, but it shows us the consistency of God's pattern of perfection in the Divine-human relationship.

God's Record. In the New Testament there are numerous aspects of man's threefold relationship with God. John spoke of "three that bear record in heaven, the Father, the Word, and the Holy Ghost: and these three are one" (1 John 5:7), and of "three that bear witness in earth, the Spirit, and the water, and the blood: but these three agree in one" (1 John 5:8).

Christian Holy Living. The Apostle Paul emphasized that Christians have a responsibility to "live soberly, righteously, and godly, in this present world" (Titus 2:12). Repeatedly we encounter this use of three qualities in God's admonitions for our living. The point I wish to make is that in Scripture the number three is a number of fullness and perfection.

Threefold Communion. Paul summarized his great discourse on Christian love with a statement of three essentials to man's communion with God. He said, "And now abideth faith, hope, charity, these three, but the greatest of these is charity" (1 Corinthians 13:13).

The Simplest Church. In many other references we can see the importance of man's threefold relationship with God. Since God is a Trinity and man is made in this triune image, it is only reasonable that the relationship of God and man will follow the same pattern. The church is the meeting place of God and man. In its simplest terms, the church is summed up in these words of Jesus: "For where two or three are gathered together in my name, there am I in the midst of them" (Matthew 18:20). If Jesus is spiritually in the midst of the church today, then it is proper to conclude that He will do everything through us, in us, and for us that He would do if He were physically upon the earth. We, as the body, must do the bidding of the Head, which is Christ.

The Three Tabernacles. You will recall that the impulse of Simon Peter on the Mount of Transfiguration was, "Lord, it is good for us to be here: if thou wilt, let us make here three tabernacles; one for thee, and one for Moses, and one for Elias" (Matthew 17:4). Impulsive as he was, Peter came very near to the truth in speaking of three tabernacles, or churches. Jesus did not build three churches, but He did build one church consisting of three elements.

THE THREE ELEMENTS

Christ has endowed His church with three necessary spiritual components. Those who call themselves Christian cannot function adequately as the body of Christ without the three, *all of the three.* These elements are: (1) Fruit of the Spirit, (2) Gifts of the Spirit, and (3) The Ministry Gifts.

These elements are not optional—they are necessary to us if we are to be what He has called us to be. Men often endeavor to function without one of the three, but this rejection or neglect leads to difficulty and trouble—or, much worse, to apostasy. The spiritual elements are given to us in order that we may be adequate for His work in our day. Each component has its particular purpose and service to the church. Nothing is given to us simply for form, but each part of the body has a vital function in the body. The lack of any one invariably leads to particular dangers and evils.

Fruit of the Spirit. First among the essential qualities of the church is spiritual fruit. Fruit is our identification as the people of God, for the fruit a tree bears is the positive proof of its species. For instance, a tree may resemble a peach tree and may even grow in a peach orchard; but if the fruit it bears is apples, then it is an apple tree. Its species is not determined by the way it looks or where it grows, but by the fruit it bears.

> Ye shall know them by their fruits. Do men gather grapes of thorns, or figs of thistles? Even so every good tree bringeth forth good fruit; but a corrupt tree bringeth forth evil fruit. A good tree cannot bring forth evil fruit, neither can a corrupt tree bring forth good fruit. Every tree that bringeth not forth good fruit is hewn down, and cast into the fire. Wherefore by their fruits ye shall know them (Matthew 7:16-20).

The Fruit of the Spirit in our lives is the proof to the world, and to ourselves, that we are the children of God (John 13:35; 1 John 3:14). In Galatians 5:22, 23 we have the best-known listing of the spiritual fruit in the lives of Christ's followers: "But the fruit of the Spirit is love, joy, peace, longsuffering, gentleness, goodness, faith, meekness, temperance: against such there is no law." These Christian virtues constitute our Christlikeness. It is by them that we reveal the nature and the Spirit of Christ. Without them we could not correctly call ourselves Christian.

Strangely, there are always some Christians who feel that they are identified by what they *do not* bear. No branch is good simply because it *does not* bear bad fruit; it is good only when it *does* bear good fruit. The incident of Jesus and the fig tree (Matthew 21:18-20; Mark 11:12-14) is a clear example of this. Jesus did not bless the tree because it did

not have poisonous, bitter, sour or shrivelled fruit on it. Instead, He cursed it because it did not bear the good fruit
that it should. In the same way, no person is good because
of the multiplicity of bad things he does *not* do; he is good
because of the good he *does*.

Jesus further emphasized this truth in His parable of the
talents (Matthew 25:14-30). In the parable those servants
who did what was good were blessed, but the servant who
tried to prove his worth by doing no wrong was cursed.

Now let me illustrate the position of the Fruit of the
Spirit in the structure of the church. It, like the symbol of
God and man, is in the form of a triad. We shall see later
that the Fruit follows the threefold pattern of perfection and
completeness in both kind and function.

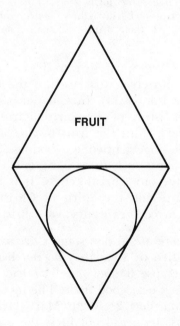

While the Fruit of the Spirit is primary and essential to the Christian's *identification,* it is not the sole element of the church. There are other essentials as well. The Fruit alone leads to *ineffectiveness* in the work of Christ. Those who exemplify only the Fruit may live a Christlike *life,* but they need a further element for doing His *work.* God did not establish His church simply to *be* good—although this is primary and absolutely essential—but also to *do* good. Through the Fruit of His Spirit we show His nature—His love, joy, peace, longsuffering, and so on—but it remains for us to do His works. If we, therefore, magnify the Fruit of the Spirit and neglect God's other gifts to the church we may be good people, but we will not be balanced and effective. Christ was not the Messiah merely because He manifested spiritual fruit; He was the Messiah because He did the work the Messiah was to do. The church will be the body of Christ only as it lives the life and does the works of Christ.

Gifts of the Spirit. For the purpose of His work, Christ has given Gifts of the Spirit to the church. These are listed in 1 Corinthians 12:8-10: "For to one is given by the Spirit the word of wisdom; to another the word of knowledge by the same Spirit; to another faith by the same Spirit; to another the gifts of healing by the same Spirit; to another the working of miracles; to another prophecy; to another discerning of spirits; to another divers kinds of tongues; to another the interpretation of tongues." As with the Fruit of the Spirit, there are nine Gifts in this list of God's endowments to His church. The Gifts are special graces or blessings given to the church for its operation as the body of Christ. Just as the Fruit of the Spirit enables us to live His life, so the Gifts of the Spirit empower us for His service. When we illustrate the place of the Gifts in the church we see how they balance and correlate with the Fruit.

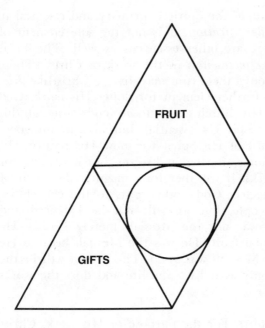

The Gifts of the Spirit must not be emphasized above the Fruit of the Spirit—and, indeed, they cannot exist without the Fruit. All who neglect the Fruit and exalt the Gifts run the danger of fanaticism and possible heresy. The two must be balanced in the Christian life. Because of the spectacular nature of the Gifts, there are some immature or zealous Christians who attempt to manifest them without appropriate cultivation of the Fruit in their lives. This cannot be successfully done and should not be attempted. No one can leap-frog over the Fruit of the Spirit into the realm of the Gifts of the Spirit. Any apparent manifestion of the Gifts without the Fruit is exactly that—an appearance, not reality. God would not give us the spiritual power inherent in the Gifts unless we were spiritually prepared and responsible through the Fruit in our lives.

With this understanding of the relationship of the Fruit and the Gifts, let me emphasize the need of the Gifts in the work of Christ. All of the Gifts of the Spirit were evident in the life of Christ, and it is only through them that we can continue His work. No one can effectively do the work of Christ without supernatural provision, for which reason we are given power by the Holy Spirit to share His understanding, do His work, and speak His words. He enables us to do on earth what He would do if He were here in body. We must be His body in essence and in power.

The Ministry Gifts. God does not indiscriminately give such power as is manifested in the Gifts. Just as there must first be worthiness and spiritual qualification through the Fruit, so there must be responsibility and appropriate regulation through His further gifts to the church. Where this regulation is ignored, the church runs into trouble. This leads us to the third element the Lord has placed in the church.

Related to the Gifts of the Spirit are the Ministry Gifts of Christ. These are particular anointings God gives to men for particular needs and aspects of His service. A list of these ministries, along with certain spiritual gifts, is given in 1 Corinthians 12:28, "And God hath set some in the church, first apostles, secondarily prophets, thirdly teachers, after that miracles, then gifts of healings, helps, governments, diversities of tongues." The list shows us that it is the Holy Spirit who gives both the Gifts of the Spirit and the Ministry Gifts. The Fruit, Gifts and Ministries are sometimes intermixed in Scriptural listings (Romans 12:4-8), which emphasizes their unison in the church—and the fact that each component is vital and assumed to be present in the work of the church. The three elements compose the spiritual equipment God has given us for His service.

In Ephesians 4:11-16 we have not only a listing of the
Ministry Gifts, but also a statement of their purpose in the
church:

> And he gave some, *apostles;* and some, *prophets;* and some,
> *evangelists;* and some, *pastors* and *teachers;* For the per-
> fecting of the saints, for the work of the ministry, for the
> edifying of the body of Christ: Till we all come in the unity
> of the faith, and of the knowledge of the Son of God, unto
> a perfect man, unto the measure of the stature of the ful-
> ness of Christ: That we henceforth be no more children,
> tossed to and fro, and carried about with every wind of
> doctrine, by the sleight of men, and cunning craftiness, where-
> by they lie in wait to deceive; But speaking the truth in love,
> may grow up into him in all things, which is the head, even
> Christ: From whom the whole body fitly joined together and
> compacted by that which every joint supplieth, according
> to the effectual working in the measure of every part, maketh
> increase of the body unto the edifying of itself in love.

Observe that ministry is vital to the thesis I have set forth:
the body of Christ, the church, is to extend from Him, the
Head, in perfect function and purpose. What Christ was on
earth, we the church must constantly endeavor to be.

The Ministry Gifts, like the Fruit of the Spirit and the
Gifts of the Spirit serve a threefold purpose in the church.
Their place in the structure of the church should be illustrat-
ed as in the facing figure.

The ministry brings the church pattern back to the original triad design, which signifies perfection, completeness,
balance. The Ministry Gifts are essential to the purpose of
the church, for without them there would be disorder and
confusion, and the effectiveness of the Fruit and the Gifts
would be compromised. Bear in mind that the purpose of
the ministry is for the perfecting, or completing, of the body
of Christ. The importance of the ministry is seen in the
completion of the church function and pattern. It is this
element that provides direction and regulation to the
church. Without the Ministry Gifts the other elements of the

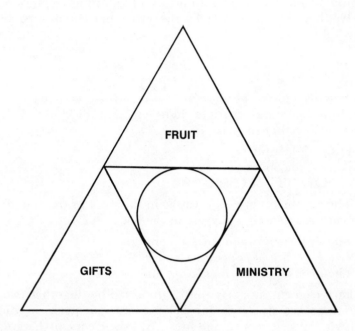

church would be ineffective through overlapping in some instances, and thinness of efforts in others.

The necessity of the Ministry Gifts is obvious. The ministry must not be ignored, but neither should it be emphasized above the Fruit and the Gifts. When the ministry is over-emphasized to the neglect of the Fruit and the Gifts, the church runs into ecclesiastical tyranny and carnal lordships. An admirable organization may be created, but its spiritual purposes are lost. The ministry can serve its purpose only as it functions in balance and harmony with the other elements of a spiritual church. It would be a doleful thing to live in a church rigid and precise in its administrative organization but without the grace of the Fruit or lacking the

power of the Gifts. The authority of the ministry is good
only when it is tempered by the Fruit and empowered by
the Gifts.

SUMMARY

Now let me recapitulate and summarize what I have set
forth in the preceding pages. Jesus endowed the church with
three essential elements:

Fruit of the Spirit
Gifts of the Spirit
Ministry Gifts of Christ

These elements are cooperative in the work of the church,
yet each has a specific purpose in the body.

The *Fruit* is for *identification* and *grace*.
The *Gifts* are for *operation* and *power*.
The *Ministry* is for *regulation* and *service*.

Each element supports and is supported by the other two.
All three are necessary for balance and adequacy in the
church. Any element alone presents a deficiency or hazard.

Fruit alone leads to *ineffectiveness*.
Gifts alone leads to *fanaticism* or *heresy*.
Ministry alone leads to *tyranny*.

When the church of God is in full possession of the elements intended for it, it is the capable and powerful body of
Christ. Its savor is good in an evil world, its function is
smooth and harmonious, and its power is adequate for its
task. Identified by the Fruit, empowered by the Gifts, and
regulated by the Ministry, the church is truly an extension of
Christ its Lord.

PART TWO

FRUIT OF THE SPIRIT

But the fruit of the Spirit is love, joy, peace, long-suffering, gentleness, goodness, faith, meekness, temperance: against such there is no law (Galatians 5:22, 23).

Whereby are given unto us exceeding great and precious promises: that by these ye might be partakers of the divine nature, having escaped the corruption that is in the world through lust. And beside this, giving all diligence, add to your faith virtue; and to virtue knowledge; and to knowledge temperance; and to temperance patience; and to patience godliness; and to godliness brotherly kindness; and to brotherly kindness charity. For if these things be in you, and abound, they make you that ye shall neither be barren nor unfruitful in the knowledge of our Lord Jesus Christ (2 Peter 1:4-8).

2
FRUIT OF THE SPIRIT

PURPOSE OF THE FRUIT

As I have noted earlier, Fruit of the Spirit is our identification as the body of Christ; it reveals to the world and to us that we are the disciples of Christ. In fact, the Fruit can be called the sum of our Christlikeness. We do not reveal Him in our lives by calling ourselves Christian, or even by obeying a set of moral laws, or by simply pretending to be like Him—we show the life of Christ by the consistent presence in our lives of "love, joy, peace, longsuffering, gentleness, goodness, faith, meekness, temperance" (Galatians 5:22, 23). Nine fruit are mentioned here, but this is not necessarily an exhaustive list. Other graces and virtues—such as hope and diligence—are also manifestations of Christlikeness, but these nine definitely summarize the body of fruit we must bear. They constitute a standard by which we can measure our likeness to Christ.

41

Peter gave a summary of Christian fruits and stated their
purpose, ". . . that by these ye might be partakers of the
divine nature, having escaped the corruption that is in the
world through lust. And beside this, giving all diligence, add
to your *faith* virtue; and to *virtue* knowledge; and to *knowledge* temperance; and to *temperance* patience; and to
patience godliness; and to *godliness* brotherly kindness; and
to brotherly *kindness charity*. For if these things be in you,
and abound, they make you that ye shall neither be barren
nor unfruitful in the knowledge of our Lord Jesus Christ"
(2 Peter 1:4-8).

We see clearly that the Christian life is to be a Christlike
life. These positive virtues are to be manifested in us or we
are not truly Christian. When men see us they should see
Christ in us, as we exemplify His nature, His spirit, and His
character. Peter called the followers of Christ "a chosen generation, a royal priesthood, an holy nation, a peculiar people;
that ye should shew forth the praises of him who hath called
you out of darkness into His marvelous light" (1 Peter 2:9).

Some seem to believe they can show Christlikeness by the
multitude of things from which they abstain. It is as if some
say, "I'm better than you because I'm against more things
than you are," or, "I'm holier than others because there are
more things I don't do than others don't do." This is erroneous and Pharisaic (Luke 18:11). Clearly there are many
sinful and worldly things a Christian should not do (1 Peter
2:11), but not committing evil is not enough: we *must do*
that which is righteous and good. It is not enough that we
do not curse—but we must bless. It is not enough that we
do not use our lips for profanity—we must use them for praise.
It is not enough that we abstain from worldly amusements
and diversions—we must participate in worship and Christian
witness. It is not enough that we do not cheat and defraud—
we must use our material benefits to assist others. It is not

enough that we do not use our money for gambling and sin—
we must use it for the extension of God's work. In short, it is
not enough that we do not bear evil fruit—we must bear that
which is good.

God said, "Be ye holy; for I am holy" (1 Peter 1:16).
Certainly no one believes that God is holy because of what
He does not do. He is holy because of who He is, what He
is, the nature of His person and His works. God is holy in
every way. It was the same with Jesus. He did not prove
He was the Son of God because of what He did not do,
because of the attractions of the world He avoided. Proof
that He was the Son of God lies in the fact that He *did* what
the Son of God was born to do. The same is true with us.
We prove our holiness by what we do, not by what we do
not do.

Nature of the Fruit

The Holy Spirit is the source of the Fruit of the Spirit.
Our Christlikeness is the consequence of His influence in our
lives, and without His influence there is no likeness of Christ.
He is the origin of all our human goodness.

Occasionally we see persons who, even though they are not
Christians, have natural dispositions or attitudes that resemble the Fruit of the Spirit. Some men are by nature more loving and more lovable than others. Some have a more peaceful
or tranquil disposition than others, and some seem more
cheerful or joyful than others. And most certainly there are
some persons who are by nature more patient and more
temperate than others.

Now it must be clearly understood that the Fruit of the
Spirit is "of the Spirit"—that is, the fruit is Spirit-originated,
Spirit-motivated, Spirit-borne. Natural tendencies, similari-
ties and approximations should never be mistaken for the

spiritual fruit. Indeed, the spiritual fruit is often contrary to the natural attitude, in that the man of God is able to love the unlovable, have joy unspeakable, and peace that passes understanding. We shall see more of these possibilities later on.

God does definitely build upon our natural gifts and faculties. For instance, a naturally joyful person will continue to be joyful—but his joy will be transposed to a higher spiritual level. Some men by nature find it easy to love others, but it is usually those who are themselves pleasant and lovable. We can love our friends and benefactors easily, but we will need more than natural love when we meet the hateful, obnoxious and cantankerous people around us. Then our natural inclination to love others will be insufficient. We will need the manifestation of the Spirit to enable us to reach such heights of love. What was evident in measure by nature will become manifest in extraordinary measure and under the most difficult circumstances when it is transposed, or lifted to a higher level, by the Spirit.

Some people endeavor to produce spiritual fruit through self-effort, by resolutions or self-reformation. But these virtues are not natural to us, and are contrasted by Paul to the works of the flesh (Galatians 5:19-21). These graces are the fruit of the Spirit's indwelling. They are not the "fruit of self," but the Fruit of the Spirit. When we give the Holy Spirit full control of our lives, when we surrender to His influence upon us, this Fruit will flourish in all nine manifestations.

THE INCREASE OF FRUIT BEARING

The influence of the Holy Spirit does not begin with the baptism of the Holy Ghost, but it comes into our lives much earlier. The Holy Spirit is active in our conversion, which is being born of the Spirit (John 3:6; Romans 8:9). Those who are "born again" will bear the Fruit of the Spirit immediately, and the Fruit will increase as we grow in Christ (1 Peter 2:2; 2 Peter 3:18). When we are baptized in the Holy Spirit our fruit-bearing will be much increased.

Jesus spoke to His disciples of first bearing *fruit*, then *more* fruit, and finally *much* fruit (John 15:2, 5). This statement not only attests to the increase of fruit-bearing in us, but it speaks of a pruning process responsible for the increase, ". . . every branch that beareth fruit, he *purgeth it, that it may bring forth more fruit*." Now this purging means cutting, or pruning, from our lives all that is unlike Christ or that hinders our fruitfulness for Him. Purging or purifying is often a painful process, but it must be done. We must be purged of our fascination with the world, our carnal ambitions, our profane associations and our own base nature, in order that Christ and His nature may abide and abound in us. If we are not purged of unspiritual attitudes and habits, then we shall die—and no fruit grows on dead branches. Then Christ shall take us away and we will lose our place in Him (John 15:6). We must therefore submit ourselves constantly to the painful but essential pruning.

God has left to us some aspects of our own purging. We need to be careful in our consideration of this responsibility, lest we come to believe that we can cleanse ourselves into a state of grace. This cannot be done. We must first be washed by the blood of Jesus Christ (1 Corinthians 6:11; Revelation 1:5; 7:14) and then His grace and strength enables us to purify and cleanse our lives. He washes away the sin that condemns us, but we must cleanse ourselves from habits and attitudes that are unlike Him. Consider the following scriptural admonitions in this regard:

> Let us cleanse ourselves from all filthiness of the flesh and spirit, perfecting holiness in the fear of God (2 Corinthians 7:1).

> And every man that hath this hope in him purifieth himself, even as he is pure (1 John 3:3).
>
> Cleanse your hands, ye sinners; and purify your hearts, ye double minded (James 4:8).
>
> If a man therefore purge himself from these, he shall be a vessel unto honour, sanctified, and meet for the master's use, and prepared unto every good work (2 Timothy 2:21).
>
> Purge out therefore the old leaven, that ye may be a new lump, as ye are unleavened (1 Corinthians 5:7).

The truth of these scriptures is that Christ cleanses us from sin and we bear His fruit. Then by submission to Him we must cultivate in our lives such purity that He can increase His nature in us. Let me repeat that we cannot do this in or of ourselves; it is by Him that we bear all spiritual fruit.

Categories of the Fruit

The Fruit of the Spirit as listed in Galatians 5:22, 23 is noted in the singular form "fruit" rather than the plural "fruits" even though there are nine. "But the fruit of the Spirit is love, joy, peace, longsuffering, gentleness, goodness, faith, meekness, temperance. . . ." The meaning is that the fruit of a Spirit-directed life will be a multiplicity of positive virtues. This points up the unity of the spiritual virtues in our lives, which are interlocked and cooperative with one another. For instance, genuine love will bring joy, and abounding joy is always a source of peace.

Just as one manifestation encourages another, the absence of one prohibits another. No one can have peace when he fails to manifest faith, or even longsuffering. And so the Fruit of the Spirit is much like one chain of nine links. Each link is separate and entire, complete in itself, and yet it is only one part of the chain, the greater whole. There is unity with a multiplicity of parts.

The nine manifestations of the spiritual fruit continue the threefold pattern we have already observed, and fall into three conspicuous groups of three. Thus we see the plan of God unfold consistently in all aspects of our Christian experience. The pattern of the Fruit is thus:

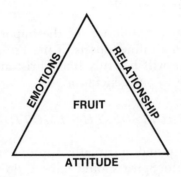

Now let us observe the distinctions and see how completely we are to be filled with and controlled by the Spirit. When we are filled with the Spirit, He will influence and control the way we view ourselves, the way we relate to our fellowman, and the way we approach God in obedience and worship. He will control the whole of our lives.

FRUIT OF THE EMOTIONS
  Love, Joy, Peace.

FRUIT OF RELATIONSHIP
  Longsuffering, Gentleness, Goodness.

FRUIT OF THE ATTITUDE
  Faith, Meekness, Temperance.

The *emotional* fruit has to do with what is inside us, our deepest personal feelings, our emotions and what those emotions cause us to do.

The *relationship* fruit has to do with our association with others, how we relate to our fellowmen, both saint and sinner, and how our lives affect them.

The *attitude* fruit has to do with our attitudes toward God, how we yield to His influences and appropriate His will and blessings to our human lives.

By looking at the nine we see the importance of each in our lives. When all nine aspects of the Fruit are fully manifested in us, we will be truly like Christ and our lives will extend His life to our generation.

FRUIT OF THE EMOTIONS

It is naturally and spiritually appropriate that the first three Fruit of the Spirit should have to do with the human emotions. The emotions are the passions, the sensibilities, the deepest feelings of a man. These are those feelings that go throughout a man's consciousness and to a great extent make him what he is. We are creatures of emotion, which means that we feel deeply and subjectively about things that touch our lives, either real or imaginary. The Holy Spirit invades the whole man and influences his deepest thoughts and attitudes; He influences the emotions and makes them good. Until this is done we have little chance of manifesting the other fruit.

Love and *hate* are two of the most passionate and important emotions. What we love and what we hate are of equal importance in the development of our character. R. A. Torrey says:

> It is not enough to love righteousness; iniquity must be hated as well. On the other hand it is not enough to hate iniquity; righteousness must be loved as well. There are those who profess to love righteousness, but they do not seem to

hate iniquity. They are strong in applauding right, but not equally strong in denouncing evil. There are also those who profess to hate sin, but they do not seem to love righteousness. They are strong in denouncing evil, but not equally strong in applauding right. Jesus Christ's holiness was full-orbed as well as spotless; He loved righteousness and hated iniquity (Matthew 17:5).[3]

Joy and *sorrow* are also contrasting emotions, and the things that bring us joy or sorrow are important to our spiritual character. All men have both emotional manifestations, but they may do so for quite opposite reasons. When the Holy Spirit possesses and dominates our lives we will express both joy and sorrow in the right manner and to the appropriate degree. The Spirit will give us balance. For example, it is quite appropriate for us to sorrow over some tragedy, and totally inappropriate to be overcome with sorrow.

Peace and *anxiety* are other emotions of opposing manifestations, as are *fear* and *courage, hope* and *despair.* One of the most important works of the Spirit in the regenerated heart is this control and influence of the way we feel about life around us. He touches and affects every fiber of our temperament and produces grace and virtue in us. All men are emotional, but happy is that man whose emotions are under the lordship of the Spirit.

The emotion of fear is a clear example of how the Spirit will control or influence the emotions. Paul wrote, "For God hath not given us the spirit of fear; but of power, and of love, and of a sound mind" (2 Timothy 1:7). Here he is speaking specifically of the emotion that destroys and torments. Yet we are told that God has put His fear in our hearts (Jeremiah 32:40). Fear in this sense is reverence or awe, an emotion that fortifies the soul and makes us acceptable to God.

EMOTIONS AND EXPRESSION

A word of clarification is necessary here, since there is some misunderstanding about what emotion is. A common mistake is that we are emotional when we express our feelings in a conspicuous manner. Some express joy by loud praise or even physical demonstration; or they express sorrow by loud weeping and wailing. The way in which the feeling is expressed is not the emotion, but a demonstration of it. Men who react to their emotions with reserve or even transfixation are fully as emotional as those who have uninhibited and physical reaction to them. The emotion is the deep feeling of the mind and soul.

I recall a time when I was a boy that two young men were walking along a railroad track near our home. A train came roaring around the bend behind the boys and bore down on them with great speed. A strong wind in their faces and the configuration of the bend kept them from hearing the warning whistle. Just before the train reached them they felt the vibration of the tracks and leaped to safety as the train thundered past them. One of the young men, realizing how narrowly he had escaped with his life, leaped and ran and whooped through the furrows of our cornfield. The second young man sank to the ground in mute shock, joy, wonder and gratitude. Both boys felt the same emotion, but they expressed it in totally different ways. It would be sheer folly to suggest that the boy who ran and yelled was more emotional than his friend—he simply expressed his emotion in a different manner. Under the stimulus of spiritual blessing I have through the years seen Christian men express the very same emotion in different ways.

Suppose that two women are bereaved by the death of a loved one. One woman may weep and talk incessantly about her loss, about her grief, and she may have such expressions of anguish that sedation becomes necessary. The second woman, on the other hand, may be so struck with sorrow that she is unable to speak or even unable to weep. Her shock may go so deep into her that she is left with mute wells of grief that defy all expression. The emotion of both women is the same; the only difference is the way each woman's individual temperament causes her to express that grief.

Emotions are involuntary—they are either present or they are not. There is very little we can do toward bringing them into being, for the more we try to do so the more we end in mental frustration. Saying you love someone you do not love is sheer mockery—you either love them or you do not. Joy, likewise, cannot be genuinely expressed by self-effort, for the more consciously we try to find joy the less likely we are to have it. And peace is driven away when we try to create our own. Those who attempt to express emotions that are not genuine usually become frustrated or neurotic. You see, emotions are our deep feelings, and efforts to create emotions are little more than surface pretenses. To create or change an emotion we must touch the depth of our lives and change the way we feel. This is by nature virtually impossible. That is why the emotional fruit is paramount in Christian living. By submitting ourselves to the Holy Spirit, He fixes in us true emotions that glorify God and edify man.

Whatever the emotion—fear, hope, courage, reverence —it is based in the spiritual circumstance of our lives. The emotions of love, joy and peace are inner qualities from which issue, or to which are related, all the emotions of life.

1. LOVE

Primary among all Christian expressions is love, a virtue with which Jesus specifically identified Himself. "This is *my commandment,* That ye love one another, as I have loved you" (John 15:12). Note that He called it a commandment and not mere advice or suggestion. Today Jesus does not say, "I strongly *recommend* that you love one another"; He requires us to emulate His love. It is clearly stated that we are to love both God and our fellowman, and what measure of love we are to have.

> Jesus said unto him, Thou shalt love the Lord thy God with all thy heart, and with all thy soul, and with all thy mind. This is the first and great commandment. And the second is like unto it, Thou shalt love thy neighbour as thyself. On these two commandments hang all the law and the prophets (Matthew 22:37-40).

Upon these two aspects of love hang all the necessary commandments. Such perfection of love makes the fulfillment of the laws of God a normal way of life. Consider how this assures our obedience of the "Ten Commandments" (Exodus 20:3-17). When we love God with all our heart, soul, mind and strength, (1) we will have no other gods before Him; (2) we will not worship idols or graven images; (3) we will not take the name of God in vain; (4) we will keep the sabbath day holy; (5) and if we love our heavenly Father as we should, certainly we will honor our earthly father and mother.

When we love our neighbor as we love ourselves we will have no difficulty in keeping all commandments that pertain to him. (1) We will not kill; (2) we will not commit adultery; (3) we will not steal; (4) we will not bear false witness against our neighbor; and (5) we will not covet that which is not ours.

And so in all of life the fruit of love makes the obedience of Divine law both natural and good. Jesus called love a *new* commandment, "A new commandment I give unto you, That ye love one another; as I have loved you, that ye also love one another" (John 13:34). Everywhere in Scripture we see the emphatic demands of love. There is no option otherwise—for love is the first requisite for Christian living. Any alternative is harsh and deadly, "He that loveth not his brother abideth in death" (1 John 3:14).

Our human love is based upon the love of God, who not only loves, but who *is* love (1 John 4:8, 11). In modern times the word "love" has largely lost its meaning because of an erroneous, maudlin, sentimental usage. Men speak of loving things and food and experiences and virtually everything that touches their lives. The word is so misused and overused that it has been emasculated and reduced to sticky sentimentality or puerile meaninglessness. When most men speak of love, at the very best they usually mean a favorable feeling of sympathy or desire. But love is real, alive and vital, an active force that acts on behalf of the one beloved. Our love is to be based upon the love of God—and every reference to His love shows Him doing something for the object of that love.

> God so *loved* the world, that *he gave* his only begotten Son . . . (John 3:16).

> Now Jesus *loved* Martha, and her sister, and Lazarus. . . . And when he thus had spoken, *he cried* with a loud voice, Lazarus, come forth (John 11:5, 43).

> Unto him that *loved* us, and *washed* us from our sins in his own blood (Revelation 1:5).

> He *loved* us, and *sent* his Son . . . (1 John 4:10).

> Christ also *loved* the church, and *gave* himself for it (Ephesians 5:25).

> He that *loveth* me shall be *loved* of my Father, and I will *love* him, and *will manifest* myself to him (John 14:21).

> For whom the Lord *loveth* he *chasteneth* . . . (Hebrews 12:6).

> As many as I *love,* I *rebuke* and *chasten* . . . (Revelation 3:19).

The list could continue to include all the references to Divine love, but that would be much more extensive than is necessary here. It is sufficient to say that in every instance of love God benefits those whom He loves—for even His chastening and rebuke are for our good.

In the same way, we are commanded to love one another; and our love, like God's, will always manifest itself in beneficial action. Love cannot remain a mere idle sentiment when there is any opportunity to act on behalf of the one who is loved. Action is implicit in Christ's statement, "By this shall all men know that ye are my disciples, if ye have love one to another" (John 13:35). If men are able to recognize us by what they witness of our love, then love is more than favorable sentiment; it is an emotion that is observable in our acts.

> Love *worketh no ill* to his neighbour . . . (Romans 13:10).
>
> He that loveth his brother abideth in the light, and there is *none occasion of stumbling* in him (1 John 2:10).
>
> . . . let us not love in word, neither in tongue; but *in deed and in truth* (1 John 3:18).
>
> Hereby perceive we the love of God, because he laid down his life for us: and we *ought to lay down our lives* for the brethren (1 John 3:16).
>
> But whoso hath this world's good, and seeth his brother have need, and *shutteth up his bowels of compassion* from him, how dwelleth the love of God in him? (1 John 3:17).
>
> Greater love hath no man than this, that a man *lay down his life* for his friends (John 15:13).
>
> . . . by love *serve* one another (Galatians 5:13).
>
> . . . have fervent charity among yourselves: for charity *shall cover* the multitude of sins (1 Peter 4:8).
>
> Charity suffereth long, and *is kind;* charity *envieth not* (1 Corinthians 13:4).
>
> [Charity] *seeketh not* her own (1 Corinthians 13:5).

In these references the focus is obviously on the love of one friend to another. It is easy to love those whom we know and like. While most men can love friends to some degree, the Fruit of the Spirit helps us to love those we have not known. The parable of the Good Samaritan was told to illustrate this very fact. We are to love, and act for the benefit of those whom God brings into the scope of our lives (Luke 10:25-37).

Beyond this, Christian love must extend even to the un-lovable. Jesus set this forth in precise terms:

> Ye have heard that it hath been said, Thou shalt love thy neighbour, and hate thine enemy. But I say unto you, Love your enemies, bless them that curse you, do good to them that hate you, and pray for them which despitefully use you, and persecute you; For if ye love them which love you, what reward have ye? do not even the publicans the same? (Matthew 5:43, 44, 46).

> But I say unto you which hear, Love your enemies, do good to them which hate you, For if ye love them which love you, what thank have ye? for sinners also love those that love them. But love ye your enemies, and do good, and lend, hoping for nothing again; and your reward shall be great, and ye shall be the children of the Highest: for he is kind unto the unthankful and to the evil (Luke 6:27, 32, 35).

This commandment to love our enemies requires sober consideration. It is not an easy commandment to obey, for it is contrary to our human reactions. Yet Jesus mentions four negative and harmful forces that mày assault us and then requires us to meet them with four positive and beneficial reactions. His demands in this regard are clear. We are required to:

Meet	ENEMIES	with	LOVE
Meet	CURSING	with	BLESSING
Meet	HATE	with	GOODNESS
Meet	PERSECUTION	with	PRAYER

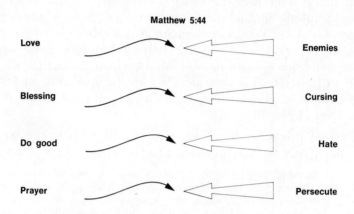

Matthew 5:44

Love — Enemies

Blessing — Cursing

Do good — Hate

Prayer — Persecute

Every natural tendency is to meet ill with ill, but Jesus says to meet evil with good. Keep in mind, however, that Jesus is speaking of actions rather than sentiments; we do not have to *like* those who hurt us—we like our friends—but we do have to love them. Our love may manifest itself in stern ways designed to bring our enemy into a better way. The test of love is in our motive. If we seek vengeance or retaliation, then we meet hate with hate, or at least with ill. When we seek the correction or ultimate benefit of those who hurt us then we demonstrate the tenacity of love. But this one thing is certain—*love will never harm,* it will always bless.

Spiritual love will inevitably lead to joy, a joy that will be realized both here and hereafter. Love is the fountain from which all other virtues of Christian living flow.

2. JOY

Second only to love is the fruit of joy, in many ways the most misunderstood and overlooked of Christian virtues. This is not due to any neglect in the Scriptures, for joy is mentioned about 150 times in the New Testament. Perhaps it is because joy is so incongruous in a day of universal sorrow and sadness. It is like an anachronism, something out of time and out of place. But this should not be so, for there have been sad times before, even sadder than our own time.

Christianity was born in the saddest of times. With the exception of the Jewish worship of Jehovah, the world was devoted to a sorry assortment of gods, demons and spirits. More than half of the world was in slavery or servitude. Most men had forgotten, if they had ever known, how to laugh. Joy and happiness were not even concepts to most men, who accepted their sadness and absence of spirit as a matter of fact. Human life itself was held in light regard, especially the lives of the enslaved and the poor.

Into such a world came the joyous tidings of Christ. He did not overlook the facts of life, but gave His followers a sense of being, a view of life that gave them joy. Joy is a pervading emotion that exists in the face of all circumstances when we are fully in accord with Christ. Our joy does not bow to situations or things for it is based upon an inner awareness of God.

There are three words that have similar but not identical meaning: *joy, happiness* and *pleasure.* It is important that we observe their distinctions. Any or all of the three may come to us in the Christian life, and all are frequently mentioned, but only joy is constant. Happiness and pleasure are both capricious and transitory, dependent upon external influences for their existence. We may experience happiness one day and unhappiness the next—or the change can easily occur in the course of a single day. Similarly, pleasure comes to us inconstantly—and is relative to our personal preferences.

Happiness is dependent upon happy circumstances and situations. We may find happiness in good company, fellowship, or family and friends, probably the greatest human sources of happiness. Let our happy situations be replaced with unhappy or lonely situations and our happiness departs. Worse still, it may be overcome by and replaced with unhappiness. What makes one person happy does not necessarily make another so. Some are happy with quiet and calm situations while others are happy with crowds and activity; some are happy in travel and others are happy when they are settled in one place. Causes of happiness are as different as the temperaments of men. God frequently gives us happy circumstances, but happiness is not an unfailing right of the Christian life.

Pleasure comes to us with pleasant things. Some find pleasure in good music, good literature, good conversation, and so on, but take away these pleasant things and pleasure is replaced with displeasure. Whatever is contrary to our personal preferences shatters our sense of satisfaction, which is the basis of pleasure.

So we see that happiness and unhappiness, pleasure and displeasure move in and out of our lives with considerable caprice, while joy is constant and enduring. Happiness is dependent upon happy situations, and pleasure upon pleasant things, but joy is dependent only upon God.

Joy is the state of well-being and assurance that makes us content even in the face of adversity. The virtue is particularly related to the fullness of the Holy Ghost (Acts 13:52). Joy is indifferent to the circumstances that determine happiness and the things upon which pleasure depends, and is frequently most apparent in the face of unhappiness and displeasure. Our joy is to be constant, and in all circumstances.

Paul directed the early church to, "Rejoice in the Lord

alway: and again I say, Rejoice" (Philippians 4:4), and encouraged the people to, "Rejoice evermore" (1 Thessalonians 5:16). In many ways, the fruit of joy is most conspicuous in times of adversity, a pattern which Jesus set when He "for the joy that was set before him endured the cross, despising the shame, and is set down at the right hand of the throne of God" (Hebrews 12:2). He showed in His crucifixion how joy can be maintained in the absence of either pleasure or happiness. This is borne out in Christ's message to those who are persecuted: "Blessed are ye, when men shall revile you, and persecute you, and shall say all manner of evil against you falsely, for my sake. Rejoice, and be exceeding glad: for great is your reward in heaven" (Matthew 5:11, 12).

Obviously there is no pleasure in persecution, but there can be joy. Nor is there pleasure in temptation and trials, but James shows how even this can be a cause of joy. "Count it all joy when ye fall into divers temptations; Knowing this, that the trying of your faith worketh patience" (James 1:2, 3). The sense of all this is that the Christian has a deep inner awareness of blessedness that surpasses his immediate surroundings. At one time when the apostles were beaten they reacted with rejoicing (Acts 5:40, 41), not because the beating was pleasant or the situation happy, but because they were aware that they suffered for Christ. This is an instance of joy's dominance over adversity. In temptation and trial we can have joy because their very presence indicates that our position in Christ is secure.

Christians can and should reflect joy in the midst of sin and ungodliness. Working or living among those who find delight in parading their evils before us is unpleasant, but even this can bring joy because of our personal freedom from such vices. Frequently, as I travel in the work of the

Lord, I am in such circumstances that I thank God that He has cleansed me from sin and secured me from addiction to the offensive liquor or tobacco or profanity or lewd conversation. I am therefore unhappy because of my present surface circumstance, but I have joy because of an awareness of deeper and more enduring circumstances.

The early Christians were a happy, joyful people and their message was one of optimism and gladness. Their lives were filled with irrepressible joy, based upon a sure confidence in Jesus Christ, "in whom, though now ye see him not, yet believing, ye rejoice with joy unspeakable and full of glory" (1 Peter 1:8).

With such hope and joy the disciples went into a world of sadness, and their joyous message won men to a better way. Pentecostal people of today have a similar opportunity to show forth the praises of the Lord Jesus Christ. Ours too is a joyous message, in a world that languishes for joy. This is a day of pervasive sadness, when men seek to cover their sadness with bizarre and garish masks and actions. Many of this day have resorted to drugs that dull reality and induce stuporific gaiety. They retreat to dark recesses of artificiality and seek joy in the gloom of smoke, the hypnosis of piercing sound and the delirium of intoxication and frenzy.

And while the world seeks for artificial gaiety we have a harvest of joy within us. When the fruit of joy abounds in our lives, it extends to all areas of living so that we find pleasure in more things and happiness in more situations. The fruit of joy helps us to see the good and delightful things of life wherever they are found.

We cannot help but have joy when we take time to consider how we are surrounded by so much that is good. For the Christian, life itself is good, and that is a cause for unending joy. The forgiveness of sin and the fullness of the

Spirit are causes for joy. Belief that Jesus rose from the dead must bring joy, as does our hope of resurrection. Belief that He stands at the right hand of the Father making intercession for us certainly gives joy. Belief that He is coming again occasions joy for those who are prepared for His coming. And belief that we shall live with Him eternally is reason for our greatest spiritual joy.

With these beliefs within us we can and should be the most joyful people on earth. Faith in Christ is a happy and joyous matter, and no circumstance can or should unsettle that experience or assurance.

3. *PEACE*

Peace in its most common sense means an absence of war and hostility, but as a Fruit of the Spirit it means much more than that and touches every part of life. It is a state of individual harmony with life, which includes God first of all, then our fellowmen, and finally ourselves. This harmony of life must reach into the deepest recesses and extend to the farthest reaches of our persons.

True peace is one of the most difficult virtues to develop and maintain. In fact, it is impossible without the nurture of Christ within us. Peace was associated with Christ's birth, when the angels sang, "Glory to God in the highest, and on earth peace, good will toward men" (Luke 2:14). It was also associated with His death, when He said, "Peace I leave with you, my peace I give unto you" (John 14:27). Observe that it was *His* peace that He left us and it is *His* peace we are expected to manifest.

The peace of Christ is not mere passiveness, complacency or absence of involvement—it is peace in the midst of conflict. Jesus lived in a time of gravest conflict and yet His life radiated absolute inner peace, and His peace was com-

municated to others. Some men seem to have the virtue
of peace only because they are unaware of the chaos and
disorder about them. The spiritual peace Christians have
should live triumphantly in the face of, and with full
knowledge of, the turmoil and confusion around them. This
is victorious Christian living; this is the Lord's intention
for His people.

In his little book on *New Testament Christianity*, J. B.
Phillips, New Testament translator and scholar, says:

> But as we study New Testament Christianity, we are
> aware that there is an inner core of tranquillity and sta-
> bility. In fact, not the least of the impressive qualities which
> the Church could demonstrate to the pagan world was this
> ballast of inward peace. It was, I think, something new that
> was appearing in the lives of human beings. It was not mere
> absence of strife or conflict, and certainly not the absence of
> what ordinarily makes for anxiety; neither was it a lack of
> sensitivity nor a complacent self-satisfaction, which can often
> produce an apparent tranquillity of spirit. It was a positive
> peace, a solid foundation which held fast amid all the tur-
> moil of human experience. It was, in short, the experience
> of Christ's bequest when He said: "Peace I leave with you,
> my peace I give unto you: not as the world giveth, give I
> unto you" (John 14:27).[4]

A man with Divine peace in his life will manifest it in
many ways, of which inner tranquillity is but one. This
fruit of the Spirit will be present as a multiple virtue of:

1. Peace with God
2. Peace with man
3. Peace with self.

Peace With God. The first of these is primary, for without harmony with God there can be no other genuine peace
in our lives. This fact is obvious when we bear in mind
that we are created in His image. No man who has discord with God can expect to find peace on any other level.

Harmony with God is implicit in Christ's analogy of the Vine and the branches. Without free flow of the Spirit and nature of God in us we have no hope of bearing His fruit. Discord with God makes inner peace impossible, and fills us with disabling anxieties and frustrations. Many a man is incapacitated by neuroses that stem directly from disunity with his Creator. Until peace is attained no other peace is attainable.

Peace with God is obtained at our conversion and is maintained by our constant submission to His will. If we try to place our own will above His will then we fill our hearts with tensions and anxieties—and the fruit of peace withers and dies. The presence of sin in our lives will destroy all possibility for this peace. A transgression may not be so grave that it alienates us from the grace of God and yet it will impair our harmony with Him. Frivolous and worldly living may not damn us but it brings discord to our peace with God and with ourselves.

Peace With Man. Peace with man is a Christian imperative. We are commanded to "Follow peace with all men, and holiness, without which no man shall see the Lord: Looking diligently lest any man fail of the grace of God; lest any root of bitterness springing up trouble you, and thereby many be defiled" (Hebrews 12:14, 15). Peter also directs the people of God to live peaceably in anticipation of the Lord's return: ". . . we, according to his promise, look for new heavens and a new earth, wherein dwelleth righteousness. Wherefore, beloved, seeing that ye look for such things, be diligent that ye may be found of him in peace, without spot, and blameless" (2 Peter 3:13, 14). It is interesting that both the Hebrews reference and that of Peter associate the word "peace" with the word "diligence." The inference is that peace is the result of persistent effort and desire. It does not always come naturally, for peace is frequently difficult to attain. This is clearly the view of Paul in Romans 14:19: "Let us therefore follow after the things which make for peace, and things wherewith one may edify another."

All men are not peaceable, yet we must endeavor to be peaceable toward them. Our responsibility is so great in this regard that we can be fully successful only when the Spirit bears His fruit freely in our lives. Only through the Spirit can we turn the other cheek as we should when every human impulse is to strike back at the one who hurts us (Matthew 5:39). There are some men who cannot get along with anyone; they have no peace with themselves and they reject all efforts of others to be peaceable with them. Our responsibility in such cases is to see that our own attitudes are right. Paul, in reference to such persons, said: "If it be possible, as much as lieth in you, live peaceably with all men" (Romans 12:18).

Peace With Self. Peace with oneself is the most difficult of all aspects of peace to maintain. The reasons are obvious, for everything about us and our relationships with others affects our inner sense of right and wrong. Discord with my neighbor, and most assuredly discord with God, also takes away peace with myself. I lose inner peace when I lose harmony on any other level. I cannot be at peace with myself until I have peace with others.

Moreover, I alone know my thoughts, my motives, and my desires. Others may see what I do, but I know why I did it. When my motives are ignoble it matters little to my peace of mind if my deeds seem noble. The praise of others cannot compensate for a disquieted conscience. I not only know *what* I did and *why* I did it, but I know what I *wanted* to do and dared not. I know what I would have done—or even might have done—if I had been absolutely sure no one else would ever know. What I *do* can destroy peace with others, but what I *think* can destroy peace with myself. Peace can be restored with myself only when I have set my values straight once again and have secured the grace of God for my mental folly.

On the other hand, we can have inner peace when we know the righteousness of our reasons even when those reasons are obscure to the eyes of those who would condemn us. "Beloved, if our heart condemn us not, then have we confidence toward God" (1 John 3:21). There may be times when we inadvertently offend others; they think we intended them harm when we know we did not. Then our only responsibility is to go to them and solicit their understanding and good will.

Peace in the Church. In the world there is strife and division without remedy, and it is in this regard that the church is most clearly distinguished from the world. Great importance is placed on peace in the church, for it is the responsibility of the church to show Christ's peace to the world. A special blessing is pronounced upon those who encourage peace: "Blessed are the peacemakers: for they shall be called the children of God" (Matthew 5:9). Paul warned of the dangers that exist when the church is divided and in conflict with itself, "But if ye bite and devour one another, take heed that ye be not consumed one of another" (Galatians 5:15).

In his excellent book on *The Christian Character,* Stephen Neill, missionary to India, makes this incisive observation:

> But the Church cannot fulfil this duty, unless it is at peace in itself. The saddest thing in the history of the Church is that Christians have found it so difficult to live at peace with one another.
>
> The Church is divided, and so it is weak. Where the Spirit rules, there is peace; the Churches will find again their lost

unity only when they are really ruled by the Spirit of God, and make the service of God their one and only aim.

But even in small Christian groups we often find strife, where there ought to be peace. It was so among the apostles; there was strife among them as to which should be the greatest (Luke 22:24). St. Paul had to appeal to two good ladies in the Church at Philippi not to quarrel (Philippians 4:2). Christians today are very much like Christians nineteen hundred years ago.

Where do these quarrels come from? Do they not arise because, like other people, Christians too often want to have their own way? We are all sure that we are right; and so perhaps, when we pray "Thy will be done," we are really saying "My will be done; help Thou my will to prevail." Sometimes we are right; but we may insist on our views in such a way as to make other people angry. And serious quarrels among Christians can arise from such tiny causes.[5]

FRUIT OF RELATIONSHIP

We come now to those Fruit of the Spirit that affect our relationship with one another. These are of great importance, for Christianity is a faith and life of fellowship and companionship, and much of the New Testament teaching is directed to interpersonal matters between believers. Our communion with Christ is intended to be shared with others. Christian mystics and recluses sometimes speak of living alone or the privacy of their faith, but this is not how faith in Christ is intended to be. It is hard to live the Christian life alone, for its very nature impels one Christian to lead another person to Christ. Christianity is a faith of togetherness.

Jesus sent His disciples out by twos (Mark 6:7), and emphasized that "Where two or three are gathered together in my name, there am I in the midst of them" (Matthew 18:20). Our spiritual fellowship is vital. One cannot read the New Testament carefully without being impressed by the emphases on how Christians should relate to one another. Among the many, observe the following scriptures:

> This is my commandment, That ye love *one another,* as I have loved you. These things I command you, that ye love *one another* (John 15:12, 17).
>
> Be kindly affectioned *one to another* with brotherly love; in honour preferring *one another* (Romans 12:10).
>
> Bear ye *one another's* burdens, and so fulfil the law of Christ (Galatians 6:2).
>
> Wherefore comfort yourselves *together,* and edify *one another,* even as also ye do (1 Thessalonians 5:11).
>
> Forbearing *one another* in love (Ephesians 4:2).
>
> Forbearing *one another,* and forgiving *one another* (Colossians 3:13).
>
> Look not every man on his own things, but every man also on the things of *others* (Philippians 2:4).
>
> Let no man seek his own, but every man *another's* wealth (1 Corinthians 10:24).
>
> By love serve *one another.* Let us not be desirous of vain glory, provoking *one another,* envying *one another* (Galatians 5:13, 26).
>
> But exhort *one another* daily, while it is called Today (Hebrews 3:13).
>
> And let us consider *one another* to provoke unto love and to good works: Not forsaking the assembling of ourselves *together . . .* but exhorting *one another* (Hebrews 10:24, 25).
>
> See that ye love *one another* with a pure heart fervently (1 Peter 1:22).
>
> And above all things have fervent charity among yourselves. . . . Use hospitality *one to another* without grudging (1 Peter 4:8, 9).
>
> All of you be subject *one to another,* and be clothed with humility (1 Peter 5:5).
>
> Confess your faults *one to another,* and pray *one for another,* that ye may be healed . . . (James 5:16).

In the light of such an array of Scripture we must see how important each Christian is to another. We should keep in mind the words of Paul to the Romans, which can be applied to our relationship with others, "For none of us liveth to himself, and no man dieth to himself" (Romans 14:7). The Spirit-filled life is one of assisting others. If we become selfish or self-centered we will be unfruitful servants of Jesus Christ.

4. *LONGSUFFERING*

In one sense longsuffering is something akin to *endurance,* in which we remain stedfast to Christ in the face of difficulty or suffering. In this sense we must not be discouraged by the trial and adversity that comes to us. The Apostle Paul was a remarkable New Testament example of this virtue. He who was highly regarded by the Jews came to be utterly despised by them for no reason except that he followed the way of Christ. It is sometimes most painful to suffer contempt and abuse after one has formerly enjoyed high esteem. In Paul's words he was "defamed . . . made as the filth of the world, and are the offscouring of all things" (1 Corinthians 4:13). Moreover, he was hungry, thirsty, reviled, persecuted, and regarded as a fool. He further enumerated his sufferings:

> Of the Jews five times received I forty stripes save one. Thrice was I beaten with rods, once was I stoned, thrice I suffered shipwreck, a night and a day I have been in the deep; In journeyings often . . . in perils of robbers, in perils by mine own countrymen, in perils by the heathen, in perils in the city, in perils in the wilderness, in perils in the sea, in perils among false brethren; In weariness and painfulness, in watchings often, in hunger and thirst, in fastings often, in cold and nakedness (2 Corinthians 11:24-27).

We must add to this list of sufferings a "thorn in the flesh" that was particularly distressing to him, a personal impediment that was not removed although he earnestly prayed for deliverance (2 Corinthians 12:7, 8). The fruit of longsuffering is seen clearly in Paul's attitude toward these afflictions: "Most gladly therefore will I rather glory in my infirmities, that the power of Christ may rest upon me. Therefore I take pleasure in infirmities, in reproaches, in necessities, in persecutions, in distresses for Christ's sake: for when I am weak, then am I strong" (2 Corinthians 12: 9, 10).

It is not enough to bear infirmity or abuse with resignation, we must do so with courage and without spiritual defeat. Longsuffering is directly related to the fruit of love, just as the various fruit are related to one another. "Charity [love] suffereth long, and is kind. . . . Beareth all things, believeth all things, hopeth all things, endureth all things" (1 Corinthians 13:4, 7).

PATIENCE

Another, and more significant, meaning of longsuffering is *patience,* as it is translated in *The New Testament in Modern English* (Phillips) and the Revised Standard Version. Men of today often overlook, or even disdain, the virtue of patience. They are always in a hurry, unwilling to wait for anyone or anything. Impatience has become a neurosis of our age, and it often intrudes into the church. This is contrary to the very nature of God, who has never moved by man's timepieces.

God heard the cry of the Israelites in Egypt and answered with the birth of Moses (Exodus 3:7-10). No less than eighty years passed in His preparation of a deliverer. At another time God answered the distress of His people with the birth of Samson (Judges 13:3-5), a period of no less than twenty years. Perhaps the most telling instance was the coming of Jesus, which occurred 2,000 years after God's promise to Abraham. It required this long a period for the world to be made ready for the coming of the Messiah. In periods of

silence it often seemed that God was doing nothing, but He
was at work all the time. "But when the fulness of the time
was come, God sent forth his Son, made of a woman, made
under the law" (Galatians 4:4).

PATIENCE WITH OTHERS

The longsuffering of God is also revealed in His bearing
long with sinners and His slowness to execute judgment on
them (Romans 2:4; 9:22). He is "slow to anger, and
plenteous in mercy" (Psalm 103:8). Except for His patience,
we would have been condemned long before we came to
Him in repentance. He "is longsuffering to us-ward, not
willing that any should perish, but that all should come
to repentance" (2 Peter 3:9).

The Spirit-filled life will produce the fruit of God-like
patience in us. In contrast to impatience and shortness of
temper, we are to "put on . . . bowels of mercies, kindness,
humbleness of mind, meekness, longsuffering; Forbearing one
another, and forgiving one another" (Colossians 3:12, 13).
The imperfections of others present to us one of our most
urgent needs for patience. Inconstant Christians who are up
and down, in and out, are a test to our patience, but we must
remember that not all men are endowed with the same
strength of resolve as others. Their greatest chance of at-
taining spiritual maturity is the longsuffering of more
mature and more spiritual Christians.

Sometimes we may have a tendency to "write off" offensive persons, but when we do we go contrary to the example
of Christ (Luke 14:9), Moses (Exodus 32:32), and Paul
(Galatians 4:19, 20), who said, "We then that are strong
ought to bear the infirmities of the weak, and not to please
ourselves" (Romans 15:1). We are to restore, not destroy,
those who are weaker Christians than ourselves (Galatians
6:1).

Many circumstances in life call for the virtue of patience. The rearing of children is one of the most important of these. Just as we wait for the birth of a child, so we must wait for his development and maturity without expecting the child to be grown up before the time. Longsuffering is put to full test when some parents are given the responsibility of caring for a retarded or afflicted child that will never bring the full reward of being an adult. Such trials can be opportunities to be uncommon examples of Spirit-filled living.

5. GENTLENESS

Next among the spiritual graces we show toward others is gentleness, which is also translated *kindness*. As is true of all the Fruit of the Spirit, this virtue is based upon the kindness of God, which is manifested to all men, not just those who are themselves good and gentle. True Christian grace is precisely that: a manifestation of good toward men who not only do not deserve it, but who do deserve severity and punishment.

Most men can be kind to those who are kind and gentle themselves—or even to those who are needy and helpless— but it requires spiritual virtue to be kind to the evil-doer, the mean and disagreeable, the spiteful and hateful man. This, however, is exactly what God does: "He is kind unto the unthankful and to the evil" (Luke 6:35). This is the very nature of God, who "maketh his sun to rise on the evil and on the good, and sendeth rain on the just and on the unjust" (Matthew 5:45). God withholds His punishment of sinners and deals with them kindly in order to bring them to repentance—else we all would have been destroyed without a chance of redemption. But He does more than exercise patience, He blesses the sinner with the good things of life, with the same sun and rain and with the same sustenance of life as He blesses the saint.

We as Spirit-led children of God must likewise manifest
our kindness to all men. In one of His most demanding statements, Jesus directed His followers to do good to those who
do evil to them. ". . . do good, and lend, hoping for nothing
again; and your reward shall be great, and ye shall be the
children of the Highest: for he is kind unto the unthankful
and to the evil" (Luke 6:35).

When we are treated unjustly our natural response is to
retaliate, get revenge in the Old Testament eye-for-an-eye,
tooth-for-a-tooth manner. But the kindness of Christ will do
good instead of evil to the offender. It is not always the
easy thing to do, but kindness in adversity is "first pure,
then peaceable, gentle, and easy to be entreated, full of
mercy and good fruits, without partiality, and without
hypocrisy" (James 3:17).

"GENTLEMEN"

Possibly the greatest manifestation of gentleness is in the
behavior of a superior to those who are subject to him.
This aspect is the most common usage of the word; it is in
this regard that we get the word "gentlemen." The mercy
of God is the basis of man's gentleness to those who are at
his mercy. God does not mete to us the deserts of our deeds,
but He withholds the penalties we deserve and deals with
us in tender kindness. When we are at His mercy He deals
with us mercifully.

I cannot show gentleness when I am at the mercy of another person, I can only accept his treatment of me. It is
when I have the advantage, the "upper hand," that I can
manifest a gentle spirit. A striking example of this is in the
Lord's story of the king who forgave the debt of his servant
(Matthew 18:23-35). When payment of the debt was required
and the servant was unable to pay, the king at first thought
to exact the harshest payment and penalty. The servant

begged for mercy and the king, touched by the plea, forgave the debt. That was an act of gentleness at a time when severity would have been appropriate. Then the servant was cast into the superior position with a fellowservant who was indebted to him. Despite the pleas of the fellowservant, he refused to show mercy and sent the poor man to the debtor's prison. When the servant had the opportunity to manifest gentleness he failed miserably to do so. "Shouldest not thou also have had compassion on thy fellowservant, even as I had pity on thee?" the king asked the servant, and then subjected him to the same harshness. The Lord has dealt gently with us, and we are expected to do so with our fellowman.

Gentleness is not softness except in the finest sense—it is kindness, kindness by one who has the power or the position to be harsh and severe. A parent can be gentle with his children, remembering that kind hands guide them and harsh hands crush them. A boss can be gentle with his employees, a creditor with his debtors, a teacher with his pupils, or anyone put by circumstance in the position of a superior. "Ye masters, do the same things unto them, forbearing threatening: knowing that your Master also is in heaven; neither is there respect of persons with him" (Ephesians 6:9).

The Fruit of the Spirit will be gentle toward all men, the deserving and the undeserving. There may be times that we must exert sternness, but this will be kind and beneficent rather than retributive and destructive. Without doubt it was the gentleness of Barnabas that helped Mark find himself when that young man failed in his service to Christ (Acts 15:37-39). Mark became a man of strength and effectiveness in the ministry of the church (2 Timothy 4:11). Like Mark, other stalwart Christians often bloom late under the gentle care of those who manifest the Spirit of Christ.

6. *GOODNESS*

Of all the spiritual virtues, goodness is the most difficult to define. It would seem that all nine of the Fruit are some form or manifestation of good. One is impressed that "goodness" is a general term used in speaking of the sum of man's virtues, that positive quality opposite to badness. It is, however, both general and specific. The idea of *being* good belongs to God, for He alone *is* good in its finest sense. Man is good by *doing* good deeds. All human goodness is predicated on God's goodness.

When the man we refer to as the Rich Young Ruler greeted Jesus as "Good Master," Jesus replied by saying, "Why callest thou me good? there is none good but one, that is, God . . ." (Matthew 19:16, 17). Jesus did not, as it appears at first glance, deny that He was good; He emphasized that He was Divine. The young man had called Jesus "Master," which meant simply "teacher," but Jesus wanted him to realize He was more than a teacher. His meaning was, "If you see that I am good, why do you not see that I am God?"

> The thought of God as good and the prominence given to "good" and "goodness" are distinctive features of the Bible. In Galatians 5:22, "goodness" is one of the fruits of the indwelling Spirit of God, and in that from Ephesians 5:9 it is described as being, along with righteousness and truth, "the fruit of the light" which Christians had been "made" in Christ. Here, as elsewhere, we are reminded that the Christian life in its truth is likeness to God, the source and perfection of all good. Second Thessalonians 1:11 regards God Himself as expressing His goodness in and through us.[6]

Man has always cherished a longing to be good, as the Psalmist gave witness, "Surely goodness and mercy shall follow me all the days of my life . . ." (Psalm 23:6). But the natural man is unable to cultivate the quality of goodness,

even though he may on occasion demonstrate a good work
or deed (Romans 7:18-21). Christians, however, are called
to be "fruitful in every good work" (Colossians 1:10). Good
works are supposed to be the pattern of spiritual living.
Goodness in Scripture is not generally thought of in the ab-
stract, a state or quality of being. It is, instead, an active
virtue manifesting itself in deeds of kindness and generosity.
Because of his good deeds toward others, a man may be
regarded as good—it is not a passive and inherent quality
of character in us.

When I was young I knew a man who always spoke softly,
never quarrelled or even raised his voice, never expressed
strong or dissenting opinion when talking to others, never
reprimanded those under his authority, and never had an
enemy. I remarked to a friend about what a "good man"
this person was.

"Yes," responded my friend, "if never doing anything,
never disagreeing with anyone and never expressing an
opinion is goodness, then he is good."

I thought much upon this statement and recognized its
truth. Good is not simply the *not* doing of wrong but it is
the *doing* of that which is beneficial and helpful—and good—
to others. We read of "following good," "performing good,"
and "abounding to every good work." The phrase "good
works" is used repeatedly in Scripture.

Good Men

The Scriptures refer to only three persons as being good
men. The first is Jesus Himself. The rich young ruler called
Him "good Master," and at His crucifixion the centurion
called Him a "righteous man" (Luke 23:47). The others
are Joseph of Arimathea and the apostle Barnabas.

By looking at Joseph and Barnabas we gain strong indication of one distinction of goodness. Joseph was called "a

good man and a just" at the time he went to Pilate and requested that Jesus be buried in his private sepulchre (Luke 23:50). It was Joseph who conferred with Jesus at night during His early ministry, and he seems to have been a believer in Christ thereafter. Our next view of him is on the occasion of his appeal to Pilate and the giving of his sepulchre for the burial. Joseph was obviously a prosperous leader of the Jews, who contributed from his estate to see that the body of Jesus was properly buried.

Barnabas was spoken of as "a good man, and full of the Holy Ghost and of faith" (Acts 11:24). He was one of the first Christians, a native of Cyprus, a man of considerable wealth. He sold his land and contributed the proceeds to the apostles for the work of the church (Acts 4:36, 37). The generosity of Barnabas established a precedent that was followed by other early Christians so that a plan of community living was initiated. It is significant that in the case of both Joseph and Barnabas we see generosity with their wealth. This connection of "goodness" with generosity is interesting. The men were not noted for an absence of evil but for the practice of good works.

The spiritual life will be one of liberality. Our material means are to be dedicated and yielded to the Lord for His service and for the benefit of our fellowman.

The spiritual life will be marked with a generosity that surpasses material liberality. We are expected to give freely of ourselves—our time, our concern, our support, our prayers, or whatever else there is of us that will benefit our fellowman. This is goodness. This is the kind of concern and love God expects one Christian to have for another, and what He expects His children to have for all men.

This is the way in which Dorcas was good. She was noted for her good works and material liberality (Acts 9:36). In writing to Timothy Paul emphasized that all women should possess such virtues of righteousness and goodness. They should be "well reported of for good works . . . have lodged strangers . . . have relieved the afflicted . . . have diligently followed every good work" (1 Timothy 5:10). The fruit of goodness is a spiritual virtue that exists through the diligent doing of good works.

FRUIT OF THE ATTITUDE

In Paul's list of the Fruit of the Spirit, the third category consists of faith, meekness and temperance. These three manifestations are seen in our approach to God, and our attitude toward Him—especially our attitude toward Him in comparison to our attitude toward ourselves. The presence of the Holy Spirit in our lives will definitely affect these attitudes and will daily influence our communication with God.

This is important, for man's attitude toward God reflects his concept of God, and determines the weakness or the vitality of his spiritual life. It can, then, be said that the Divine-human encounter is the whole essence of Christian living. The fabric of our spiritual experience is woven of our relationship and communication with God.

In faith, meekness and temperance we see the subjugation of the self-life and the exaltation of the Spirit within us. No man is truly spiritual as long as he depends upon himself and his human strength or ability more than he depends upon God. His confidence must be in God and his resources must be spiritual.

Faith in God will produce faithfulness for God. There is a constant struggle in man to put trust in himself rather than in God. The Spirit has not won His victory in our lives, and therefore does not bear His fruit, until we come to full recognition that God is everything and without Him we are nothing.

In each of the three spiritual qualities that reflect our attitude we see some aspect of the human-spiritual conflict. Unless the three abound in our lives we fall short of being the spiritual persons God expects us to be. As long as we rely upon ourselves more than we do upon Him, the flesh and not the Spirit is dominant in our hearts. When the Spirit is dominant our faith will be in Him, we will be meek before Him, and we will control the self so that He may be exalted.

The infilling of the Spirit is the Christian's assurance against the inclinations of self. Even when we are saved from the works of the flesh (Galatians 5:19-21), we must still guard against the enthronement of the self. Paul, in the context of his list of the Fruit of the Spirit, said, "Walk in the Spirit, and ye shall not fulfil the lust of the flesh. For the flesh lusteth against the Spirit, and the Spirit against the flesh: and these are contrary the one to the other: so that ye cannot do the things that ye would" (Galatians 5:16, 17). Writing to the Christians in Rome he also pointed out the conflict that exists between the Spirit and the flesh. "For if ye live after the flesh, ye shall die: but if ye through the Spirit do mortify the deeds of the body, ye shall live" (Romans 8:13).

Men by nature are self-willed, self-centered, self-indulgent, self-loving, self-exalting and self-dominated. Life in the Spirit is directly opposite to this, for it centers in our correct attitudes toward God and evaluation of self. Our confidence is in Him, and in ourselves only as we are strengthened by Him (Philippians 4:13).

7. FAITH

Of all spiritual graces, faith is first in evidence in the Christian life. It must be present for a man to become a

Christian, "For by grace are ye saved through faith; and that not of yourselves: it is the gift of God" (Ephesians 2:8). Yet we find it listed seventh among the nine graces to be manifested in our spiritual lives. This placement in no way relates to its relative importance to us, for it is of primary importance—and then more.

Faith is the only quality that is mentioned as both Fruit of the Spirit and a Gift of the Spirit (1 Corinthians 12:9). This double identity requires some examination.

KINDS OF FAITH

There are four ways in which faith appears in our lives. First, there is *intellectual faith,* which is merely mental assent to the fact that there is a God. This kind of faith is held by almost everyone who lives except the most confirmed atheist. Even the demons believe this much (James 2:19). While this degree of faith is important it is insufficient, because no transformation of heart is associated with it; it is simple agreement with the *fact* of God. It is therefore no great matter when one boasts that he believes in God.

Second, there is *saving faith,* by which a soul is transformed from a sinner to a child of God. Faith is a saving power in our lives when we become convinced that God lives and that He loves us and will redeem us from sin. This is the initial act of faith, as we believe that He is merciful and faithful to forgive our sins. "For by grace are ye saved through faith; and that not of yourselves: it is the gift of God" (Ephesians 2:8). This is also embodied in the great chapter on faith in the book of Hebrews: "Without faith it is impossible to please him . . ." (Hebrews 11:6).

Third is *living faith,* which is listed as a Fruit of the Spirit. This is constant and pervasive and manifests itself day by day in every area of the Christian experience. Repeatedly in scripture we are told that "the just shall live by faith" (Romans 1:17; Galatians 3:11; Hebrews 10:38). In its deepest sense, this is that manifestation of faith without which it is impossible to please God. We pray, believing that He will hear and answer; we believe that His word is true; we believe that He sees our deeds and will reward us according to them. Every aspect of our lives is influenced and elevated by this quality of the faith and the Spirit in us.

Fourth, there is what I will call *intercessory faith*. This is the Gift of the Spirit as distinct from the Fruit of the Spirit. As we shall see later, one function of faith is when one person is enabled to believe for another. This is not living faith, which each person must have for himself, but a special anointing that comes in times of urgent need.

There is a fifth occurrence of the word "faith" in scripture that needs to be observed. It is *"the faith,"* meaning the body of truth held and propounded by the church. In this regard Christians should strive together "for *the faith* of the gospel" (Philippians 1:27); they should "contend for *the faith*" (Jude 3); and "keep the faith" (Revelation 14:12; 2 Timothy 4:7).

We can see by the numerous kinds of faith how important the virtue is in our lives for Christ. It begins with even the *desire* to know God and continues in increasing measure as we grow stronger and deeper in Him. "If ye have faith as a grain of mustard seed, ye shall say unto this mountain, Remove hence to yonder place; and it shall remove; and nothing shall be impossible unto you" (Matthew 17:20). Faith is a spiritual virtue that becomes a dominant force in our hearts. Simple faith is that which goes unchallenged by controversy, but there is also a militant faith that stands firm in the face of doubt. An unlettered man may have faith because he does not know the reasons for doubt. But there are those who know the odds and the contrary circumstances and still believe. This can only come as the Spirit manifests faith through us.

FAITHFULNESS

There is yet another way in which to view "faith," as a Fruit of the Spirit. Several modern language translations use the word "faithfulness," in which the meaning is not that we have faith but that we be worthy of the faith and confidence of others. This meaning is not that we trust God, but that we can personally be trusted. Both emphases are correct, for a man who has stedfast faith in God is certainly worthy of the confidence of others.

God needs men whom He can trust. Job is a good example of this: he trusted God absolutely (Job 13:15), and God in return trusted him with the fierce trial that came upon him. The meaning of the entire drama around Job is that God was willing to trust His servant to be faithful in the most adverse of circumstances. The same kind of Divine trust is seen in Jesus' words to Simon Peter: "Simon, Simon, behold, Satan hath desired to have you, that he may sift you as wheat: But I have prayed for thee, that thy faith fail not: and when thou art converted, strengthen thy brethren" (Luke 22:31, 32).

The gospel must be entrusted to faithful men, as must all the work of the Lord. He trusts us to be examples of His grace and stewards of His kingdom. Without question a consequence of the Spirit's indwelling will be such spiritual trustworthiness. By the Holy Spirit within us we will have such faith in Him that He can in return put trust in us.

8. *MEEKNESS*

Like faith, meekness is a fruit of our spiritual attitude, with some very important distinctions. Faith is believing God

to be what Scripture declares Him to be. Meekness is understanding the distinctions between God and self, and main-
taining a correct regard for His superiority and our
inferiority.

Meekness and humility have much the same meaning in
our lives and the words are difficult to separate in the Scriptures. Both signify man's abject regard for himself in comparison to God, and man's awareness of his utter dependence
upon God. Meekness seems to go further than humility to
include also our attitude toward other men.

TOWARD GOD

To begin with, let us see the highest manifestion of meekness. The devout holiness leader Andrew Murray said:

> Humility, the place of entire dependence on God, is from
> the very nature of things, the first duty and the highest vir-
> tue of the creature, and the root of every virtue. And so
> pride, or the loss of this humility, is the root of every sin
> and evil. . . . Without this there can be no true abiding in
> God's presence, or experience of His favor and the power of
> His Spirit; without this no abiding faith, or love, or joy, or
> strength. Humility is the only soil in which the graces root. . . .
> Humility is not so much a grace or virtue along with others; it
> is the root of all, because it takes the right attitude before
> God, and allows Him as God to do all.[7]

Meekness, then, is a sense of utter dependence upon God.
It goes against the sense of pride and self-sufficiency so dear
to the carnal mind. It is the root-soil of all holiness, for it
casts us empty and dependent at the feet of God. Meekness
is that attitude that says, "I recognize my own unworthiness
and God's perfection. I am nothing, but He is everything.
Without Him I can do nothing, but in Him I can do His
perfect will." The demands and rewards of meekness are

established in the Old Testament and carried forth with additional emphasis in the New:

> But the meek shall inherit the earth; and shall delight themselves in the abundance of peace (Psalm 37:11).
>
> Blessed are the meek: for they shall inherit the earth (Matthew 5:5).
>
> For thus saith the high and lofty One that inhabiteth eternity, whose name is Holy; I dwell in the high and holy place, with him also that is of a contrite and humble spirit, to revive the spirit of the humble, and to revive the heart of the contrite ones (Isaiah 57:15).
>
> Wherefore lay apart all filthiness and superfluity of naughtiness, and receive with meekness the engrafted word, which is able to save your souls (James 1:21).
>
> But sanctify the Lord God in your hearts: and be ready always to give an answer to every man that asketh you a reason of the hope that is in you with meekness and fear (1 Peter 3:15).

From these verses we see that the basic meaning of meekness has to do with man's attitudes toward God. Meekness, or humility, is not necessarily a sense of failure or sin; it is not synonymous with discouragement or defeat. It is rather a right estimate of ourselves in relation to our God. Tryon Edwards expresses it well, "True humility is not an abject, groveling, self-despising spirit; it is but a right estimate of ourselves as God sees us."[8]

Phillips Brooks stated this important truth in a most impressive way: "The true way to be humble is not to stoop until you are smaller than yourself, but to stand at your real height against some higher nature that will show you what the real smallness of your greatness is."[9]

God expects us to be humble and submissive to Him in order that we might measure to the full stature of His will for us. We must reach to the highest heights we can for Him, without forgetting in word or thought that it is He who wills to do, and not ourselves. He is all; we are nothing

except vessels yielded to His service. "God resisteth the
proud, and giveth grace to the humble. Humble yourselves
therefore under the mighty hand of God, that he may exalt
you in due time." (1 Peter 5:5, 6).

Toward Man

Another aspect of meekness, and an important one, is our
attitude toward others. The demands of God in this regard
are many. The Spirit will no more manifest an attitude of
haughtiness and arrogance toward men than it will an
attitude of self-will and self-sufficiency toward God. Pride
is wrong whether it is toward God or man. We must see
our fellowmen as creatures of God fully as much as ourselves. Paul said, "For who maketh thee to differ from
another? and what hast thou that thou didst not receive?
now if thou didst receive it, why dost thou glory, as if thou
hadst not received it?" (1 Corinthians 4:7).

Such meekness strikes at the very heart of our self-exalting
attitudes. It is strange indeed that some of those who *profess*
the most of holiness *possess* the most of pride. They have
pride of ability, pride of position, pride of station, pride of
possessions, pride of attainments, and ironically, pride of
holiness. They look at their fellowmen with an attitude that
says, "See, I am better than you. I have more of grace than
you. I have authority over you. I am superior to you." It is
an insidious form of pride that swells itself in an arrogant
love of self, a self-love that is willing to abuse or misuse
others in the name of holiness. This self-righteousness was
the sin of the Pharisees.

Such attitudes, spoken or unspoken, are hostile to holiness,
for there is no true holiness without humility. Jesus Himself
said, ". . . whosoever will be great among you, shall be your
minister: And whosoever of you will be the chiefest, shall be
servant of all. For even the Son of man came not to be min-

FRUIT OF THE SPIRIT

istered unto, but to minister, and to give his life a ransom
for many" (Mark 10:43-45).

Once again I quote from Andrew Murray, one of the early
leaders of the Holiness Revival in South Africa. In his excellent book, *Humility: The Beauty of Holiness,* he wrote:

> We speak of the Holiness movement in our times, and
> praise God for it. We hear a great deal of seekers after
> holiness and professors of holiness, of holiness teaching and
> holiness meetings. The blessed truth of holiness in Christ,
> and holiness by faith, are being emphasized as never before.
> The great test of whether the holiness we profess to seek or
> to attain, is truth and life, will be whether it be manifest
> in the increasing humility it produces. In the creature, hu-
> mility is the one thing needed to allow God's holiness to
> dwell in him and shine through him. In Jesus, the Holy one
> of God who makes us holy, a divine humility was the secret
> of His life and His death and His exaltation; the one in-
> fallible test of our holiness will be the humility before God
> and men which marks us. Humility is the bloom and the
> beauty of holiness.
>
> The chief mark of counterfeit holiness is its lack of hu-
> mility. Every seeker after holiness needs to be on his guard,
> lest unconsciously what was begun in the spirit be perfected
> in the flesh, and pride creep in where its presence is least
> expected.[10]

MEEKNESS IS NOT WEAKNESS

Men of humility are not proud, arrogant or egotistical.
They have a correct understanding of how they relate to the
sovereignty of God and a right opinion of themselves and
other men. They are willing to let God be their defense and
avenger. This is an important point. Humility of soul makes
us willing to leave our cause and our destiny in the hands
of God. We will not fight or scrap in our own interests.
"Speak evil of no man, to be no brawlers, but gentle, shewing
all meekness unto all men" (Titus 3:2).

Some men interpret the demands of meekness to be demands of weakness. This is not the case. Meekness is something infinitely more than weakness. It is a sign of strength borne of self-control and submission to God when men take personal abuse without striking back. This is exactly what Jesus commanded when He said, "But I say unto you, That ye resist not evil: but whosoever shall smite thee on thy right cheek, turn to him the other also" (Matthew 5:39).

This does not mean that we are to be craven or debased, without human spirit or dignity. I submit to you that meekness and humility often require the greatest kind of strength —inner spiritual strength and resolve. We need not be downcast or hangdog; spiritual men should stand erect, shoulders back, heads up, without whining or complaining, in the face of whatever abuse befalls us. Bowed in heart before God we can stand in serene dignity before men.

Meekness is not proved by pious speech or bent posture; it is proved by our attitude toward God and our fellowmen. I have seen a lot of pious pretense in my lifetime—those who, like the Pharisees, try to show their humility through soft or whining speech or clasped hands and stooped shoulders. Then I have seen those same persons manifest in conference or stress attitudes of obstinancy, doggedness and vituperation, insistent upon their own way at any cost. To them there is no consideration except to get their own way, regardless of what it does to others or even to the truth. This is pride of the worst sort, for it hides behind a mask of meekness. Let me emphasize what Andrew Murray said, "The chief mark of counterfeit holiness is its lack of humility."

Jesus. There are three in Scripture who clearly exemplify the nature of meekness—Jesus, Moses and the apostle Paul. Jesus said, "for I am meek and lowly in heart . . ." (Matthew 11:29). The meekness of Jesus was seen in His attitude toward God (John 5:30; Luke 22:42; Philippians 2:8) and

His dignified behavior before His accusers (Matthew 27:11-14). Jesus was certainly no coward. He had spoken sharply to the Pharisees, "Woe unto you scribes and Pharisees, hypocrites" (Matthew 23:13 ff), and had twice driven money changes from the Temple in the most vigorous fashion (John 2:13-16; Matthew 21:12, 13). Some may doubt that Jesus would have used His whip of cords but the money changers who saw Him had no doubt about His intent. They saw Him and fled to safety.

Moses. The meekness of Moses is mentioned in Numbers 12:3, "Now the man Moses was very meek, above all the men which were upon the face of the earth." Moses' meekness is seen in his right attitude toward God. He never forgot that he was nothing and God was everything. Not even the adulation or constant complaining of the Hebrews could turn his heart from this correct understanding (Exodus 4:10). The account of Moses' life is filled with references to his prayers to God for guidance and help. Yet this Moses became so indignant with the Israelites when they made an idol in the wilderness that he ground it into powder, poured the dust onto a pool of water and made the people drink it (Exodus 32:20). This by the meekest man on earth!

Paul. The Apostle Paul was a marvelous example of what meekness is in a man's life. He never failed in complete surrender and obedience to God; he never forgot that he was nothing and Christ was all. "Now I Paul myself beseech you by the meekness and gentleness of Christ, who in presence am base among you, but being absent am bold toward you" (2 Corinthians 10:1). Meek as he was, Paul was anything but weak. Like Moses and Jesus, he had occasions of indignation in which he rebuked or withstood many who were enemies of the gospel, as when he dealt severely with Elymas (Acts 13:9, 10), Ananias (Acts 23:3), and others.

SUMMARY

I do not make these points to suggest that we assail men with corded whips, force them to drink polluted water, or scathe them with our words. I merely wish to show that meekness is first of all our utter dependence upon God for strength, for wisdom, for holiness and for our very lives. It is furthermore an attitude of preference for our spiritual brethren and concern for all men.

Although Jesus, Moses and Paul acted or spoke with indignation on occasion it was never in a personal pique, a flare of temper, or for personal interests. In each instance they reacted to a perversion of righteousness. More than that, each of them demonstrated the most unusual love and humility on record. Moses prayed an extraordinary prayer for the very Israelites he compelled to drink the polluted water. When God would have exterminated the people, Moses prayed, "Oh, this people have sinned a great sin, and have made them gods of gold. Yet now, if thou wilt forgive their sin—; and if not, blot me, I pray thee, out of thy book which thou hast written" (Exodus 32:31, 32).

Paul had a similar love for the Jews of his day, "For I could wish that myself were accursed from Christ for my brethren, my kinsmen according to the flesh" (Romans 9: 3). He, like Moses, spoke sharply because he loved profoundly. Like parents, each man chastised the people he loved —loved so much that he would die for them.

Jesus was the perfect example of the meekness of love. He did in fact what Moses and Paul said they would do— He gave Himself for the redemption of the people. "He humbled himself, and became obedient unto death, even the death of the cross" (Philippians 2:8).

Our meekness should be the same. But that is difficult, far too difficult for natural man to attain. Meekness is a

Fruit of the Spirit and it can be borne in our lives only by the Spirit. It is by the Spirit that we see God as He is and ourselves as we are beside Him. With this right understanding our affairs will be right toward all men.

9. TEMPERANCE

We come now to the third Fruit of attitude, which is the last of the nine Fruit of the Spirit. It is different from the other eight fruit in several ways. It is the only physical virtue listed, all of the others being matters of the spirit. Examination, however, will reveal that it also is a spiritual matter.

First, let us look at temperance as an attitude. Faith is a human attitude directed altogether toward God, for faith is in Him alone. Meekness is an attitude expressed toward both God and our fellowman. Temperance is the physical fruit of a mental attitude we manifest toward God and ourselves. By the practice of temperance we are able to express our devotion to God and demonstrate respect for our own lives. To disregard temperance is to disregard a necessary spiritual truth and fail to accord our bodies an appropriate place in spiritual living.

The importance of temperance is made evident by the many times it is emphasized as a requisite for spiritual living. Both Paul and Peter list it among the Fruit of the Spirit (Galatians 5:23; 2 Peter 1:6), and Paul instructed Christians to be "sober, just, holy, temperate" (Titus 1:8). Unfortunately, in our time men associate temperance only with moderation in the use of alcoholic beverages. This is possibly due to Paul's admonition to the Ephesians, "And be not drunk with wine, wherein is excess; but be filled with the Spirit" (Ephesians 5:18).

Paul was drawing a distinction between the hilarity of

intoxication and the spiritual joy of Christian living. He went on to say, "Speaking to yourselves in psalms and hymns and spiritual songs, singing and making melody in your heart to the Lord; Giving thanks always for all things unto God and the Father in the name of our Lord Jesus Christ" (Ephesians 5:19, 20).

Naturally we must guard our lives from the abuses of strong drink, and the way to do this is to practice total abstinence. Don't drink intoxicating beverages at all. The virtue of temperance is much more comprehensive in its meaning than some have ever considered. It touches the whole of our lives. The meaning of Paul in Ephesians 5:18, 19 is that we should not allow any physical excess to deprive us of spiritual fullness. The conflict between the flesh and the spirit is great and unending, so great in fact that physical fullness often leads to spiritual emptiness. If this is the case, it is clearly better for us to be spiritually full and physically empty.

Role of the Body

The body is important in our spiritual welfare, much more than a fleshly housing for the soul. As I have pointed out earlier our body is a third part of the image of God. While we live on earth we must be concerned with and motivated by our physical selves, for separation of the flesh and the spirit on earth can never be successful. The spirit and the body are bound together, they influence one another, catch one another's diseases and share in the same determinations of life. Yet they struggle against one another in an unending spiritual conflict. The Christian concern is that the spirit be dominant over the flesh, so that our lives will extend beyond physical life. We can succeed in spiritual dominion only by being full of the Spirit, which is why temperance, or control of self, is a matter of the Spirit.

The body is never ignored in the Word of God but its purity is linked with that of the soul. Paul said, "And the very God of peace *sanctify* you wholly; and I pray God your whole *spirit* and *soul* and *body* be preserved blameless unto the coming of our Lord Jesus Christ" (1 Thessalonians 5:23). And in another place he called upon Christians to ". . . present your *bodies* a living sacrifice, *holy,* acceptable unto God, which is your reasonable service" (Romans 12:1).

Probably the most graphic reference to the necessity of keeping our physical body under the control of the Spirit is Paul's comparison of the Christian life to an athletic contest (1 Corinthians 9:24-27). He writes that "every man that striveth for the mastery is *temperate* in *all* things." The analogy is first to a foot race and then to physical combat, such as boxing or some other contest of reflexes and strength. Those who win in such athletic competition must exercise self-control and moderation in every area of their lives. Although they train diligently, some combatants will still suffer defeat, for only one can win. Not so with the Christian life, however, for all can win in it. "But I keep under my body, and bring it into subjection: lest that by any means, when I have preached to others, I myself should be a castaway" (v. 27). If our bodies control our lives, then we are carnal (for the word *carnal* means "flesh"), but if the Spirit controls the body we are spiritual.

TEMPLE OF THE HOLY GHOST

Nothing stresses the need of physical temperance and purity more than the fact that the body is the temple of the Holy Ghost. "What? know ye not that your body is the temple of the Holy Ghost which is in you, which ye have of God, and ye are not your own? For ye are bought with a price: therefore glorify God in your body, and in your spirit, which are God's" (1 Corinthians 6:19, 20). Oh,

what a wonderful truth this is. Our human bodies, frail in
one way and stubborn in another, are the abiding place of
the Third Person of the Trinity. He fills us, empowers us
and controls us—spirit, soul and body. If the body is the
temple of the Holy Ghost then it is of infinite concern
to Him that we keep His temple in purity and proper order.

REASONS FOR TEMPERANCE

Temperance should be exercised as a tribute to God, not
as mere physical deprivation. It represents a conquest of the
self-life and an exaltation of the Christ-life within us. By
temperance in all things we show our acceptance of the fact
that the spiritual life is superior to the physical.

It is difficult to see an indulgent, self-gratifying person
as a truly committed child of God. It is apparent that they
are under the control of their flesh instead of the Spirit.
Like Esau, many a potential prince of God has forfeited or
compromised his influence with God and for God by over
indulgence of his carnal cravings.

Paul mentioned temperance in all things, not merely the
filling of the body. Gluttony is obvious sin, as are greed and
covetousness, which are carnal yearnings that are superflu-
ous, inordinate or downright illegal. Most assuredly, physical or material surfeiting of any kind is contrary to the
spiritual life for it fastens us to the world and makes us
overly conscious of the carnal life (Luke 21:34). But there
are other excesses that impair our effectiveness as well. Un-
controlled emotions—anger or fear, for instance—are not
in keeping with the Christian witness. When we fail in self-
control we also fail in the ability to influence others for
Christ.

Recreation is an example of those things that in moderation are beneficial but in excess are hurtful. Some men

become slaves to the pleasant activity they intended to use as a means of relaxation and personal renewal. On the other end of the spectrum is the physical abuse of ourselves through overwork. Sometimes even this is an occurrence of pride in our lives; we can become proud of our busyness for the Lord. The harried, hurried, too-busy man is never at peak efficiency; he sacrifices effectiveness for abundance. This too is intemperance.

I remember once when as a young minister I became so exhausted that I was, for all practical considerations, drunk with fatigue. I drove myself beyond the limits of physical endurance by a too-rigorous schedule, and then went more than three days and nights without sleep in an effort to keep up with the demands that fell upon me. I lost all possibility of efficiency and almost robbed God of a usable vessel when I came to the point of collapse. That too was wrong and could have been tragic.

The lesson became clear to me: any intemperance is wrong because it reduces something God needs from us. We can only lose when we are intemperate—we lose influence, time, effectiveness, health, or attention to the spiritual life. Temperance in all things benefits us in all things.

FASTING

The utmost expression of physical temperance is fasting, those times of physical deprivation when we sacrifice all nourishment in order to attain the spiritual victory or state we need. Fasting is an acknowledgment of our bodies as the temple of the Holy Ghost. It is a conditioning for spiritual growth, an encouragement to faith and meekness. "But as for me . . . I humbled my soul with fasting; and my prayer returned into mine own bosom" (Psalm 35:13).

There is a spiritual victory, Christ said, that comes only

through prayer and fasting (Matthew 17:21). On this point John Wesley made the following observation:

> Yea, that blessings are to be obtained in the use of this means, which are not otherwise attainable, our Lord express-ly declares in His answer to His disciples, asking, "Why could not we cast him out? And Jesus said unto them, Because of your unbelief: for verily I say unto you, If ye have faith as a grain of mustard seed, ye shall say unto this mountain, Remove hence to yonder place; and it shall remove; and nothing shall be impossible unto you. Howbeit, this kind" of devils "goeth not out but by prayer and fasting." (Matthew 17:19 &c.)—These being the appointed means of attaining that faith whereby the very devils are subject unto you.[11]

It is contrary to natural reasoning to deplete oneself of physical strength at a time when it is needed most. But instead of physical strength, we are filled with spiritual victory and strength that carnal men know nothing of.

The Bible is filled with accounts of fasting. There were fasts in times of national distress, fasts for personal needs, for spiritual purification, or as expressions of remorse or grief. As Arthur Wallis has observed:

> Among great Bible saints who fasted were Moses the lawgiver, David the king, Elijah the prophet, and Daniel the seer. In the New Testament we have the example of our Lord as well as of His apostles. It clearly had its place in the life of the early churches. Nor was this biblical practice confined to men, for we find the names of Hannah in the Old Testament and Anna in the New in the ranks of the intercessors who fasted as well as prayed.[12]

I believe firmly in the effectiveness of fasting. For years I have resorted to it in times of need and times of spiritual leanness. Not once have I been disappointed. It is God's plan, asserted in His Word and honored by His Spirit. Its practice will fix the human mind and spirit on eternal rather than temporal matters; it empties self in order that Christ may be all.

SUMMARY

Now we have concluded our survey of the Fruit of the Spirit and very much is left wanting to be said. But let us look at the Fruit again—

LOVE	GOODNESS
JOY	FAITH
PEACE	MEEKNESS
LONGSUFFERING	TEMPERANCE
GENTLENESS	

Each fruit is a jewel in the crown of godliness. Take one away and you spoil the beauty of the whole. Each fruit is separate and yet it is only a part of a larger glory. Together the nine fruit comprise the highest expression of a holy life.

PART THREE

GIFTS OF THE SPIRIT

Now there are diversities of gifts, but the same Spirit. And there are differences of administrations, but the same Lord. And there are diversities of operations, but it is the same God which worketh all in all. But the manifestation of the Spirit is given to every man to profit withal. For to one is given by the Spirit the word of wisdom; to another the word of knowledge by the same Spirit; To another faith by the same Spirit; to another the gifts of healing by the same Spirit; To another the working of miracles; to another prophecy; to another discerning of spirits; to another divers kinds of tongues; to another interpretation of tongues: But all these worketh that one and the selfsame Spirit, dividing to every man severally as he will (1 Corinthians 12:4-11).

3

GIFTS OF THE SPIRIT

POWER FOR SERVICE

Having surveyed the Fruit of the Spirit, we need to bear in mind that these virtues, basic as they are to Christian living, do not represent all that God has provided for the church. A person may consistently manifest all the Fruit of the Spirit in his life so that he is a good man indeed, and still come short of what God wants His people to be. The Fruit are only one aspect of life in the Spirit. In addition to those graces by which we exemplify the nature of Christ, God has given special gifts to the church in order that the works of Christ can be done. Christ specifically stated that His followers would do His works after He returned to heaven (John 14:12; Matthew 28:19, 20).

We cannot do the works of Christ by human strength, so Christ has given us the necessary spiritual power for the task. In Acts 1:8 He said, "But ye shall receive power, after that the Holy Ghost is come upon you: and ye shall be wit-

nesses unto me both in Jerusalem, and in all Judaea, and
in Samaria, and unto the uttermost part of the earth." The
special enduement of power was an infilling of the Holy
Spirit which Jesus frequently promised His disciples during
His last days with them. After this infilling the disciples
were able to continue the work of Christ with remarkable
similarity. They preached the Word with boldness, they
healed the sick, they cast out devils, they exhibited uncommon courage and wisdom, and fulfilled the commandments of Christ in their work. They became in reality an
amplification of His voice and an extension of His hands.

The point must be kept in mind that the baptism of the
Holy Spirit is not conversion, it is a spiritual anointing and
infilling that comes only to those who are already converted.
It does not add to the Christian's state of grace or make
him holy. He can receive the blessing only when he has
been cleansed by Jesus' blood. The Baptism is a power for
Christian service, an enablement for the work of Christ.

In 1 Corinthians 12:7-10 Paul enumerates nine spiritual
gifts that are provided by the Holy Spirit for the work of
the church. These gifts are just as essential for Christian
service as the Fruit of the Spirit are for Christian living.
Any church that endeavors to function as the body of Christ
without claiming and exercising the Gifts is incomplete and
out of balance. We must have both the Fruit and the Gifts,
which both complement one another and serve distinct
functions in the witness of the church.

THE PENTECOSTAL MOVEMENT

Sometime after the days of the apostles the church diminished its emphasis on the spiritual gifts and scriptural reference to them was passed over as being outdated. Most of
the Gifts were regarded as something that had served their

GIFTS OF THE SPIRIT

purpose and were ended. Occasionally through the centuries some small group of Christians realized that the spiritual gifts were still the heritage of the church and laid claim on them. These occasions were generally shortlived and widely scattered.

Near the turn of the twentieth century there were outpourings of the Holy Spirit in numerous parts of the United States, Europe and other parts of the world. The local outpourings spread, flowed together and merged until they became a worldwide spiritual renewal. The name "Pentecostal" was given to the revival movement because the spiritual experience the people received almost exactly duplicated that of the disciples on the Day of Pentecost.

The baptism of the Holy Spirit and the Gifts of the Spirit were prominent features of the Pentecostal Revival. The Pentecostals insisted that the spiritual renewal was for all people, intended for all who call themselves Christian. For years, however, the only appearances of the spiritual phenomena occurred within the Pentecostal ranks.*

At about the midpoint of the twentieth century the Pentecostal message began to have effect in the established denominations. Ministers and members of these churches experienced the infilling of the Holy Spirit and spoke with tongues. There were miraculous healings and other spiritual works among the people. Because the Greek word for "gift" is *"charisma"* this reclamation of the Spirit Gifts came to be known as "The Charismatic Renewal." In most parts of the world today the Pentecostal Revival and the Charismatic Renewal have brought a recurrence of apostolic fervor with apostolic power.

*I have discussed the history and beliefs of the Pentecostal Movement in much greater detail in my earlier books, *Like a Mighty Army* and *The Pillars of Pentecost.* Readers desiring further details in this area are directed to those earlier works.

Before we examine the individual Gifts of the Spirit, it is well for us to analyze certain general points that demand understanding. The devil was not able to hold back the revival and its truth, so he would now like to make it unacceptable because of error and misunderstanding. What the devil cannot defeat he endeavors to confuse. The Gifts of the Spirit are too important to the life and function of the church to be overlooked or ignored, so it is absolutely necessary for us to understand what the Gifts are, what is their nature, and what is their purpose.

THE GIFTS AND THE FRUIT

The Gifts of the Spirit cannot work independently of the Fruit of the Spirit. Since both are manifestations of the same Spirit they will at all times be in agreement with and complement one another. We must bear in mind that the Fruit of the Spirit precedes the Gifts of the Spirit. It is error to imagine that anyone can bypass the Fruit and receive the Gifts. The Fruit has to do with our lives, the way we live, the way we relate to our fellowman, and the way we show the nature of Christ. It is the Fruit of the Spirit that identifies us as the children of God.

The Gifts of the Spirit are given for Christian service, to enable us to do the works of Christ. While both Fruit and Gifts are necessary for a balanced church, the Fruit is primary and the Gifts attend the Fruit. A man may be a Christian without claiming the Gifts, but he cannot be a Christian without bearing the Fruit. Such a state would make him powerless and ineffective to a great degree, but it would nevertheless be possible. But it would not be possible for him to manifest the Gifts without bearing the Fruit.

The Fruit of the Spirit, the Gifts of the Spirit and the Ministry Gifts are frequently intermixed in scriptural list-

ings. We find instances of this in Romans 12:6-13 and
1 Corinthians 12:28-13:13. This mixed listing verifies that
Fruit, Gifts and Ministry originate in the same Spirit and
are expected to be manifested in unity in our lives. The
Fruit, the Gifts, and the Ministry cannot contradict one
another, but they must function in agreement and balance
in the church.

The primacy of the Fruit over the Gifts is everywhere established in Scripture, but nowhere more emphatically than
in 1 Corinthians 13. In that great chapter Paul shows that
the fruit of love is the fountainhead of other fruit, such as
peace (v. 5), joy (v. 6), longsuffering (v. 4), gentleness
(v. 4), goodness (v. 5), faith (v. 7), meekness (v. 4) and
temperance (v. 3). Viewing the Fruit as a single element
embodied in love, Paul asserts this as being superior to the
Gifts in Christian living. He mentions or alludes to five
of the gifts in his comparison: tongues, prophecy, word of
wisdom, word of knowledge and faith (vv. 1, 2). This entire section of Paul's epistle was written to emphasize the
necessity of giving the Fruit prominence over the Gifts. "But
covet earnestly the best gifts: and yet shew I unto you a
more excellent way" (1 Corinthians 12:31).

Christ and the Gifts

In His earthly life Jesus manifested all spiritual gifts fully.
It would be erroneous to say that He manifested the Gifts of
the Spirit as such, just as it would be erroneous to say that
He lived a Christian life. *We* live a Christian life when we
pattern ourselves after Him, and *we* manifest gifts of the
Spirit when we do the works He has called us to do. Jesus
did that which was natural for Him to do.

During the days of His incarnation Jesus relied upon God
the Father and the power of the Spirit as we must do in
our lives for Him. It is said that He was *"led* up *of the spirit*

into the wilderness" (Matthew 4:1); He said "I cast out
devils *by the Spirit* of God" (Matthew 12:28). Jesus clearly
taught that the Father was the source of His power during
His days on earth. As our example He submitted Himself
to the will of the Father and the empowering of the Holy
Spirit.

> Then answered Jesus and said unto them, Verily, verily, I
> say unto you, The Son can do nothing of himself, but what he
> seeth the Father do: for what things soever he doeth, these
> also doeth the Son likewise. For the Father loveth the Son,
> and sheweth him all things that himself doeth: and he will
> shew him greater works than these, that ye may marvel. I
> can of mine own self do nothing: as I hear, I judge: and my
> judgment is just; because I seek not mine own will, but the
> will of the Father which hath sent me (John 5:19, 20, 30).

After the Passion of Jesus, when He had secured the salvation of mankind by obedience to the Cross, He said, "All
power is given unto me in heaven and in earth" (Matthew
28:18). All power had belonged to Jesus from the beginning, but He had to rely upon the Father and the Holy
Spirit during the days of His incarnation. "Until the day
in which he was taken up . . . he *through the Holy Ghost*
had given commandments unto the apostles whom he had
chosen" (Acts 1:2). Before His ascension Jesus gave promise to His disciples that they should also receive power
from the Holy Ghost. The meaning becomes very clear: the
church of Jesus Christ can draw from the same source of
power that belonged to Him while He was on the earth.

Where Are the Gifts

A question of great importance regarding the Gifts of
the Spirit is the manner in which they are gifts. In our
culture a gift belongs to the receiver, or else it is no gift
at all. There must be no strings attached or we regard that
it is not truly a gift. This is not the scriptural view of

gifts, but that of Western man. For example, a friend may give me a necktie with the sincere belief that I will wear that tie to worship services and other suitable functions. I am not bound to use it in that manner, however, and could wear the tie to places of sin and debauchery. More than that, if I so chose I could actually hang myself with it. The point is that once the friend has given me the tie it becomes mine to use in what way I will.

This is certainly not God's way of giving, for all His gifts are with condition. His gifts are for a sacred purpose and if that purpose is profaned then the gift is withdrawn. In all cases the Lord retains the power of His gifts and extends the benefits of them to His people. This in no way suggests whim or caprice on the part of God, but it emphasizes His sovereignty and Divine responsibility.

Concerning the Gifts of the Spirit, Paul stated that "The *manifestation* of the Spirit is given to every man" (1 Corinthians 12:7). He further said that "God hath set some in the church" (1 Corinthians 12:28). The meaning of this seems to be that the spiritual gifts are resident in God, set in the church, and manifested through individuals. The nine gifts are set in the church for the benefit and edification of the kingdom of God and are manifested through individuals as it pleases Him. In reality all nine of the gifts should be operating freely in every congregation of the people of God.

There is never any justification for an individual to claim that *he* possesses any particular gift, meaning, "This belongs to me. God gave it to me and it is mine." If it belonged to him in the way I have mentioned that modern man views gifts, then the individual could use the gift at his own discretion in his own way, however unwisely or carnally. God is not so irresponsible as to give gifts in this

fashion. He retains the power of the gifts and manifests
them through individuals as He will.

In a splendid little book entitled *Manifestations of the
Spirit* by R. E. McAlister, we find this point emphasized.

> Resident in the Triune God, these gracious favors are nat-
> urally classified in a threefold grouping. They are gifts, ad-
> ministrations, and operations. They naturally are associated
> with the Father, the Son, and the Holy Ghost. Since the Holy
> Ghost is the active Agent of the Godhead, it is only natural
> that these favors come to the believer as manifestations of
> the Spirit (1 Corinthians 12:7). These manifestations are
> ninefold (1 Corinthians 12:8-10). The first two namely: the
> word of wisdom and the word of knowledge, are definitely
> attributes of God. "In him dwelleth all the treasures of wis-
> dom and knowledge."
>
> The very nature and character of these attributes of God,
> which are resident in Him, forbids the theory that they are
> given, received, imparted or confirmed in the believer as a
> permanent gift, to be used at will. The Bible furnishes mul-
> tiplied evidence that they were experienced in times of need
> and emergencies, in life and ministry. The teachings and in-
> structions and incidents of God's Word reveal them as avail-
> able when needed and as occasion served. These gracious
> attributes of God come to the believer as manifestations of
> the Spirit in times of need. Spirit-filled believers have po-
> tentialities for them as they yield to God in an attitude of
> faith. God, Who is sovereign, in His good pleasure divideth
> them severally as He wills.[13]

If I could lay claim upon some gift of the Spirit as though
it were mine, that it belonged to me, that I possessed it,
then I would be at frequent variance with the Fruit of the
Spirit. I am in harmony with the Holy Spirit only when
I recognize that I bear the Fruit as the Spirit enables me
and I manifest the Gifts as the Lord imparts the manifestation to me. I know that it frequently appears that some
individual possesses a particular gift, especially when he is
repeatedly used for a particular manifestation. For example,

a person may be used so frequently with the gift of healing that it seems as though that gift belongs to him. To all intents and purposes that is correct, but the person himself must never be carried away with false notions of personal possession. He must bear in mind that the gift is in God's hand and God is merely manifesting it through him. This understanding is the very point of the fruit of meekness in our lives.

I think I can explain this with an illustration about the house I live in. I am a minister and the church I serve provides me a very comfortable and suitable parsonage. It is the place for which I become homesick when I am away. It is the home where I can rest and find comfort. It feels like my home and seems like my home. If you should ask one of my neighbors, "Whose house is that?" he would reply, "That house belongs to Mr. Conn." The neighbors think of it as my home and it serves every function of a private home, but I know that that house is provided for me by the church in order that I might do the work of the church. I know the distinctions; I know that it is not my home at all; I know that the benefits and provisions are mine so long as I am faithful in the labor to which I am called. But let me undertake to use that home for a sinful purpose and all would see that it is not mine at all: it belongs to the church I serve, although its use and benefits belong to me.

If I as an individual should have in my personal possession the gift of healing then I would be of no service to God when the need is for the gift of interpretation. The gift of tongues would be of little use to me if I were standing before a tribunal of gospel-haters and needed a word of wisdom. That is why God retains possession and control of the gift and imparts to the individual the needed manifestation.

How Gifts Are Given

An erroneous belief that could well do injury to the truth concerns the manner in which gifts are given. Because of misunderstood scriptures, some Pentecostals have concluded that human beings can bestow spiritual gifts. I have visited meetings where this travesty has actually been attempted. It is utter folly for one individual to attempt to bestow a gift of the Spirit upon another. This error arises from a misunderstanding of Paul's statements to Timothy, "Neglect not the gift that is in thee, which was given thee by prophecy, with the laying on of the hands of the presbytery" (1 Timothy 4:14). "Wherefore I put thee in remembrance that thou stir up the gift of God, which is in thee by the putting on of my hands" (2 Timothy 1:6). Paul also wrote to the church in Rome: "For I long to see you, that I may impart unto you some spiritual gift, to the end ye may be established; That is, that I may be comforted together with you by the mutual faith both of you and me" (Romans 1:11, 12).

Attentive reading of Paul's words to both Timothy and the Romans will show that there is no reason to believe that he is positing that an individual can bestow a gift of the Spirit upon another. The instructions to Timothy clearly relate to the ministry gift of an evangelist. Frequently the Ministry Gifts are affirmed by the laying on of hands (Acts 13:2, 3), which signifies the church's recognition of the ministry to which God has called an indivdual.

There are also accounts in Scripture of the laying on of hands for the Holy Ghost baptism (Acts 8:17, 18). This was done in a gesture of encouragement and support in prayer, without intimation that the Holy Ghost was given by the apostles. The simple truth is that God gives the manifestation of spiritual gifts to "every man severally as he will" (1 Corinthians 12:11).

In writing to the Romans Paul in no way suggested that he would bestow on them a Gift of the Spirit. He referred to a mutual gift of fellowship in the Word that he might share with the Romans. "That is," he said, "that I may be comforted together with you by the mutual faith both of you and me." He gave the spiritual gift of the Word to the Romans. In return they gave him the gift of fellowship and comfort.

How "Greater Works" Are Done

One of the most misunderstood scriptures of the New Testament is Jesus' reference to "greater works" in John 14:12: "Verily, verily, I say unto you, He that believeth on me, the works that I do shall he do also; and greater works than these shall he do; because I go unto my Father." Through a misunderstanding of this verse, there have been some who have discouraged true faith or have gone into fanaticism. All sorts of aberrations can result when men believe that they are called upon to exceed the miraculous works of Christ. Such belief results in unnecessary discouragement and frustration or harmful error.

The key to interpretation rests in the meaning of the word "greater." The word has two meanings and it is important for us to know which Jesus intended. In one sense the word "greater" refers to *kind* or *quality:* one thing can be of greater quality than another. For instance, a Cadillac is a greater car than a Volkswagen. In another sense the word "greater" refers to *scope, size* or *extent.* For example, a man of seventy years has had a greater lifespan than a man of twenty years; a man of two hundred pounds is of greater weight than a man of one hundred pounds; and fifty miles is a greater distance than twenty. A careful reading of Jesus' statement makes it clear that this is the sense in which He meant "greater works."

It is impossible to do a greater *kind* of work than Jesus did, for in the spiritual realm He forgave sins, a work we are unable to do. In the physical realm He raised the dead to life again, and no physical work could ever exceed that. In the sense of greater *scope* or *extent*, however, we are able to exceed the works of Christ. He made the statement at a time when He was facing death and would terminate His work on earth. He gave this as the basis for His statement, "because I go unto my Father." In years of activity, number of converts won, number of miracles performed, number of miles traveled, and number of hearts reached with the gospel we may exceed what Christ was able to do in His three and a half years on earth.

Now let us look at what His work was. In Luke 4:18, 19, Jesus used a portion of the prophecy of Isaiah to signify the nature of His work: "The Spirit of the Lord is upon me, because he hath anointed me to preach the gospel to the poor; he hath sent me to heal the brokenhearted, to preach deliverance to the captives, and recovering of sight to the blind, to set at liberty them that are bruised, To preach the acceptable year of the Lord."

In Luke 19:10 He said: "For the Son of man is come to seek and to save that which was lost." All else in Christian service must be supportive to this purpose. Whatever manifestation of gifts there may be, it must in some way assist in the high purpose of preaching the gospel and winning the lost to Jesus Christ.

THE INTERMIXING OF THE GIFTS

The nine Gifts of the Spirit frequently work in cooperation with each other. It is very unusual for any manifestation to stand alone. As it was with the Fruit of the Spirit, the Gifts are interlocked, cooperative, working toward one end.

Obviously the word of wisdom and the word of knowledge are frequently manifested together. The gift of interpretation can only operate in conjunction with the gift of tongues. The discerning of spirits becomes essential for the gifts of healing and the working of miracles. The gift of faith will work in cooperation with all of the others. The Gifts are not given to be isolated units, but they stand as one unit of spiritual power and energy.

The interworking and overlapping of the Gifts will be seen clearly as we look at them individually. We will also see their unity as well as their diversity. Once again let me draw an analogy to a chain. Each of the nine links is separate, complete in itself, and yet each is linked to another, so that the nine units constitute one whole.

CATEGORIES OF THE GIFTS

Following the great design of the Trinity we have already discussed, we now find that there are three categories of the Gifts of the Spirit. In diagram the Gifts would look like this:

Each of the three categories consists of three gifts, in this order:

GIFTS OF REVELATION
Word of Wisdom
Word of Knowledge
Discerning of Spirits

GIFTS OF OPERATION
Faith
Gifts of Healing
Working of Miracles

GIFTS OF INSPIRATION
Prophecy
Tongues
Interpretation of Tongues.

These are the nine gifts listed in 1 Corinthians 12:8-10, which substantially and practically include all the *charismata,* or Gifts of the Spirit. In Scripture there are other references to spiritual manifestations, but these generally fall into the categories listed above. At least for the purposes of our study we will look at Paul's concise enumeration of the Gifts.

GIFTS OF REVELATION

By means of the three gifts of revelation God imparts to man something of His own omniscience. By them at times He reveals His own infinite mind to the finite mind of man. Jesus probably gave promise of these gifts as much as any other before He left His disciples (read Luke 21:12 ff), because He knew there would be times of uncertainty and bewilderment when His disciples would need to know what was the will of God. How often in human life we long for a voice to show us the way. The promise of God is that "thine ears shall hear a word behind thee, saying, This is the way, walk ye in it, when ye turn to the right hand, and when ye turn to the left" (Isaiah 30:21).

Frequently in Christian living, and especially in Christian service, we need the advantage or benefit of Divine understanding. By a word of wisdom, a word of knowledge or the discerning of spirits the Lord provides such understanding to His people.

1. WORD OF WISDOM

Foremost among the spiritual gifts is the word of wisdom, which is appropriate for a quality so greatly emphasized in the Scriptures. In Proverbs we are told that "Wisdom is the principal thing; therefore get wisdom: and with all thy getting get understanding" (Proverbs 4:7). "The fear of the Lord is the beginning of wisdom: and the knowledge of the holy is understanding" (Proverbs 9:10). "He that getteth wisdom loveth his own soul" (Proverbs 19:8). Naturally these scriptures speak of human wisdom, the ability to apply knowledge and understanding to the affairs of life.

The manifestation of the Spirit called the "word of wisdom" provides understanding, solution and direction when occasions arise that require it. We are not to understand that God gives us a package of wisdom that makes us thereafter supernaturally wise. The expression "word of" signifies the spontaneous and temporary nature of the spiritual manifestation. The gift is not *wisdom* but a *word of wisdom*. The manifestation comes to us at the time and occasion when we need it.

As was explained in our discussion of the Fruit of the Spirit, this manifestation is the supernatural work of the Holy Spirit. There are men, even carnal men, who possess exceptional natural wisdom and become noted as being wise and understanding. This is not what "the word of wisdom" means. The word of wisdom is a spiritual impartation that brings edification to the body of Christ.

In Luke 21:12-15 we have the statement of Jesus regarding a primary function of the gift. When Christians are brought before magistrates and tribunals to be intimidated and persecuted, there is no need to determine beforehand what answer shall be given. "For," Jesus promised, "I will give you a mouth and wisdom, which all your adversaries shall not be able to gainsay nor resist" (v. 15). This happened often in the life of the Lord Himself, and the apostles were also frequently tried before religious councils and civil tribunals.

R. E. McAlister tells of a time when in England it was forbidden by law to gather for worship or even to read the Bible. The only legal worship was that of the state church. A young woman was on her way to secret worship when she was stopped by a soldier who demanded to know where she was going. A statement that she was on her way to worship, or to the reading of the Scriptures, would have resulted in her arrest. She breathed a prayer and the Holy Ghost illuminated her mind with the truthful answer she should give. Manifesting a word of wisdom she said, "I am going to my Father's house. My Brother died and His last will and Testament is to be read this morning. There is a legacy left for me in His will." The soldier tipped his hat and let the lady pass with a statement that he hoped there would be something good for her in her brother's will.[14] The woman went her way unhindered. She had been "wise as a serpent and harmless as a dove."

The word of wisdom frequently comes to Christians in times of danger. One of our young Spirit-filled ladies has related to me how one day when she was at work in her kitchen she felt a strong impression to stop and pray. Desiring to complete her chores she undertook to pray as she worked. The word came to her more insistently, "Stop now and pray." Unable to resist or defer the urgent voice within her she laid her dishcloth aside and went into a private room where she always prayed. She latched the door behind her out of habit, as she regularly did to keep from being interrupted. She had hardly knelt to pray when she heard someone enter the home and walk from room to room. The door of the room where she was in prayer was tried but the person, finding it locked, made no effort to force it open. With the house apparently empty, the intruder left.

The intruder went into a neighboring home where the woman was not a Christian, sensitive to the leading of the Spirit, and assaulted her. The neighbor was raped and murdered, which would have been the fate of the Spirit-filled lady except for God's word of wisdom to her.

2. WORD OF KNOWLEDGE

The word of wisdom and the word of knowledge are closely related, as are natural wisdom and natural knowledge. Knowledge is an awareness of facts and situations as they are. Wisdom is knowing how to utilize those facts to greatest advantage. In his study of the Gifts of the Spirit the late beloved Donald Gee said, "Wisdom is greater than knowledge because knowledge is not active and directive in itself. Mere knowledge in itself is of little practical value unless it is rightly applied, and this principle is just as true in spiritual things as in every other realm. This is the reason why highly educated people in the natural, and believers with a lot of Bible knowledge in the spiritual, can sometimes do extremely foolish and fanatical things. They have plenty of knowledge, but lack the wisdom to use it rightly. Very often folk with quite a limited amount of knowledge possess a rich store of genuine wisdom."[15]

In the manifestation of the Gifts God intends the word of knowledge and the word of wisdom to be cooperative. They go hand in hand, with each encouraging and completing the other. There are many times when one is manifested alone, but it is more frequent that they operate together. The word of knowledge reveals certain facts necessary and important for the work of the kingdom, and the word of wisdom generally shows how to apply this knowledge for the edification of the church.

Knowledge and wisdom joined together when it was revealed to Ananias that Saul of Tarsus had been converted to Christ and was now in the city of Damascus. Ananias went to Saul, prayed for him, encouraged him, and God's greatest missionary was launched into the service of the Lord (Acts 9:10-19). Knowledge and wisdom worked together in the revelation to Simon Peter that Gentiles could be brought into the kingdom of God. Peter obeyed the revelation and went to the household of Cornelius in Caesarea. He preached the gospel to Cornelius and his family, thereby opening the door to Gentile evangelism (Acts 10:9-48). Knowledge and wisdom worked together when Paul was on the storm-tossed ship enroute to Rome. The word of knowledge revealed that there would be a shipwreck and the word of wisdom warned that only those who stayed with the ship would be saved (Acts 27:22-31). It was the word of knowledge that manifested to Agabus that Paul would be apprehended in Jerusalem and would be delivered by the Jews to the Gentiles (Acts 21:10, 11).

A pastor friend of mine related to me a dramatic account of how the word of wisdom and word of knowledge worked in his life. A lady whose husband was an unbeliever was converted and received the baptism of the Holy Spirit. The sinner husband was angered that his wife had begun attendance at a Pentecostal church and his anger grew into hatred. The man devised a plot in which he would kill his wife and the pastor, whom he held to be responsible for his wife's change. He called the pastor and said his wife was sick and wished the pastor to come and pray for her. On his way to the home the pastor suddenly realized that something was wrong and that he should not enter the home. He felt a strong impression that the husband had become deranged and meant to do him harm. It proved to be correct. The husband had a gun with which he intended to kill his wife and the minister and then claim that he had caught them in an illicit liaison. The minister subsequently learned the details of his danger, but at the time he could only rely upon the word of knowledge and the word of wisdom as they were manifested to him.

In my own ministry there have been many occasions when these gifts have been in great evidence. These flashes of knowledge and understanding have come in numerous ways and under assorted circumstances. A particularly graphic incident happened when I was elected General Overseer of the Church of God. The General Assembly of the Church was in session and I was to be presented as moderator of the vast conference. During prayer in my hotel room the night preceding my presentation I suddenly knew that an attempt would be made the next day to disrupt the proceedings, frustrate the Assembly and put it into disorder. I somehow knew just what would happen and what the unfortunate consequences would be. That was a word of knowledge that came to me. I then prayed for God to show me what to do and while praying I miraculously knew how I must handle the situation. With that understanding I went to the Assembly early the next morning and found the potential mischief already at work. A man was on the platform busy with a scheme of disruption and disorder. I handled the matter in the way God had showed me the evening before and none of the ten thousand delegates ever knew what disorder had threatened. It was a clever device, but it was providentially revealed in time to avert it. The only thing that I did not know the evening before was who would be involved, and all I do not know today is whether it was motivated by mischief or ignorance. It does not matter, for the Spirit of God intervened for the edification of His people.

3. DISCERNING OF SPIRITS

The third gift of revelation is one which enables the believer to recognize demonic agencies. There are sicknesses caused by demon influence and sickness that is simply the result of natural causes. The gift of discernment enables us to know demonic affliction from natural malady.

I think it is appropriate to observe here that it is completely erroneous to believe that all sickness is caused by demon possession. This is a strange assertion for those who claim to be Spirit-filled. It is a vestige of the superstition of the Middle Ages, when every ill and unpleasant circumstance was attributed to Satan's influence. There is nothing more tragic than for a Spirit-filled believer to spend his days in fear that a devil might take possession of him. It is absolutely sinful for preachers to create such a spirit of fear and dread. The Word of God is precise and definite when It says "Greater is he that is in you, than he that is in the world" (1 John 4:4). No devil can take possession of that which has been purchased with the blood of the Lord Jesus Christ.

Men sometimes cite Matthew 12:43-45 as proof that a Christian can be demon-possessed. Let us look at that scripture carefully:

> When the unclean spirit is gone out of a man, he walketh through dry places, seeking rest, and findeth none. Then he saith, I will return into my house from whence I came out;

and when he is come, he findeth it empty, swept, and garnished. Then goeth he, and taketh with himself seven other spirits more wicked than himself, and they enter in and dwell there: and the last state of that man is worse than the first. Even so shall it be also unto this wicked generation.

Attention to what the scripture really says will make it clear that it does not refer to a person from whom demons had been expelled by the power of God. The demon said, "from whence *I came* out," indicating that his departure had been voluntary. He referred to the person's heart as "my house," which establishes that he had never relinquished possession. Most certainly the man's heart had not become the temple of the Lord (1 Corinthians 6:19). When the demon returned with his seven fellows he found the man's heart "empty, swept and garnished." Garnished means that it was decorated. If he had found it occupied by the Lord, washed by His blood, and used in His service, it would have been impossible for the demon and a thousand companions to force entry into it.

I have been asked in Bible conferences if it is not possible for demons to possess a Christian's body even though they cannot possess the soul. Certainly not, for the body belongs to the Holy Ghost. "What? know ye not that your body is the temple of the Holy Ghost which is in you, which ye have of God, and ye are not your own? For ye are bought with a price: therefore glorify God in your body, and in your spirit, which are God's" (1 Corinthians 6:19, 20).

When the Holy Spirit possesses my body it is most certain that He will not share His possession with demons. A child of God may be buffeted by Satan as Paul was when he had a thorn in the flesh (2 Corinthians 12:7), but no demon can ever possess or take ownership of a child of God. Any illness that can be cured by surgery or medical treatment is a natural illness rather than demon possession. Demons cannot be expelled from human lives by penicillin, streptomycin or sulfa drugs; they cannot be cut out by a surgeon's scalpel or burned out by radiation. Demons belong to the spirit world and only the power of the Holy Spirit can cast them from the human life. As long as Christians live in the world they will be subject to illness, injury and even death.

Recently I was in Seoul, Korea, to attend the Pentecostal World Conference, when a very dear personal friend, Dr. Lewis J. Willis, and I were victims of a freak accident. A bus propelled a large metal pole against us and both of us were painfully injured. Fragments of metal from the pole pierced my arm and it became badly infected. Soon my arm was greatly swollen and inflamed so that I had to be hospitalized in Hong Kong. I had blood poisoning and pseudomonas, which required immediate surgery. The Christian surgeon prayed with me and then with skillful hands cut away the infected tissue that threatened my life. Recovery was rapid from that time onward.

Make no mistake about it, no demon entered my arm with that contaminated metal and the resulting infection. Nor could one have. I am a child of God and my body is the temple of the Holy Ghost. Even with Christians natural sicknesses come and go, sometimes disappearing of themselves, and it is absurd to imagine that demons capriciously enter and leave our bodies. Such belief makes a mockery of the power of God and does despite to the Holy Spirit.

The world is filled with natural sickness, disease and affliction. There are also sicknesses and afflictions caused by demon possession. A child of God is subject to sickness that is in the course of nature, but he is not subject to demon possession. Unregenerate men are subject to both, for they do not enjoy the protection of grace. This is the principal way in which the discerning of spirits operates. Suppose that two men need prayer for apparently identical afflictions, but one is natural and the second is caused by an unclean spirit. Through the gift of discernment God will reveal that the natural sickness will require an act of healing, while the other is caused by demon possession and will require the working of a miracle.

OTHER DISCERNMENTS

The discerning of spirits will also reveal when a person's sinful state is the work of demonic possession or a simple unregenerate heart. I recall an occasion in which I was speaking to a large audience on the Christian's supremacy over devils. In the course of my message a young girl afflicted with epilepsy screamed out in the audience and hurled obscene accusations and challenges toward me. Her voice had a totally different quality from what it normally had. It would have been easy for any Spirit-filled Christian to recognize that her affliction was caused by a demon within her. The pastor of the church and I went to her, laid hands on her and rebuked the devil. He came out of the girl and she was healed, so that her life became a beautiful example of God's grace. It is futile to pray for the healing of one who is possessed of a demon, because it requires a miracle of the Holy Ghost to exorcise a demon.

There are other ways that the discerning of spirits works for the Spirit-filled Christian. A scriptural example is found in Acts 13 when Paul encountered Elymas, the sorcerer. When this renegade Jew withstood the Word of God Paul, ". . . filled with the Holy Ghost, set his eyes on him, And said, O full of all subtilty and all mischief, thou child of the devil, thou enemy of all righteousness, wilt thou not cease to pervert the right ways of the Lord?" (Acts 13:9-10).

Paul discerned that Elymas was possessed of the devil and dealt with him according to that knowledge. It was also discernment that helped Peter to know that Simon the sorcerer was "in the gall of bitterness, and in the bond of iniquity" (Acts 8:23). But Simon was an evil charlatan, not a Christian brother who had erred in the way.

By the manifestation of discerning we can also know whether our prayers are delayed because the devil hinders them (Daniel 10:12, 13) or whether God declines to grant our requests.

It is a dubious thing, and can be downright destructive, when meddlesome busybodies pretend to discern "evil in the camp." It is very easy to disturb conscientious and over-sensitive souls by suggesting to them that a revival is hindered because there is an unworthy person in the church. All sorts of confusion may result from such unscriptural and unfeeling inferences. Acting upon such suggestion in an effort to be conscientious, many persons search themselves trying to find out if they are the "Achan in the camp."* We must be very careful lest our irresponsibility create confusion in the body of Christ. His gifts and manifestations are too precious and too valuable for anyone ever to resort to pretense regarding their operation.

THE GIFTS OF OPERATION

I have designated faith, the gifts of healing, and the working of miracles as "gifts of operation" because of their active nature. While the former three reveal necessary understanding to the body of Christ, these gifts of operation are dynamic and manifest themselves in the performance of observable acts.

---

*All Israel was defeated at Ai because one man, Achan, violated God's commandment when Israel earlier defeated Jericho (Joshua 7:1-26).

4. *FAITH*

Faith is the only Gift of the Spirit mentioned also as a Fruit of the Spirit. I have pointed out certain distinctions between them in the section on "Faith" under the Fruit of the Spirit. Fruit-faith is the ordinary faith necessary for living the Christian life. Gift-faith is something quite different, for it is faith that is as miraculous and dramatic as any other gift of the Spirit. It is a faith of power and action that comes to us as a Divine manifestation in times of particular needs. We no more have it present in us every moment than we have a word of wisdom acting every moment of our lives, or no more than we speak with tongues every time we make a statement. Like all the other gifts, the gift of faith comes to us at special times as a direct manifestation of God's Spirit to meet special needs in the body of Christ. It is generally exercised in an intercessory manner, in one Christian for another.

We can no more develop this kind of faith than we can develop the word of wisdom by the practice of acting wisely, and no more than we can develop the interpretation of tongues by studying foreign languages. We can increase our fruit-faith by the practice of trust and confidence in God and by the acceptance of His will. The gift-faith comes to us when God manifests it at His will.

Let me give you an example of how the gift of faith worked in my own life several years ago. My five-year-old daughter suffered a cut on her foot while playing with her brothers and sisters on the lawn. Four days later she became desperately ill while the family was visiting in Atlanta, Georgia. Her body was twisted grotesquely and her face wore a sardonic grimace. Within an hour she began to have convulsions, during which she gnawed her tongue terribly and bled at the mouth. My wife and I took her to a hospital to have her condition diagnosed, for we feared that she might have some contagious disease that would spread to the other children. After examination the doctor announced:

"Your daughter has tetanus poisoning and is dying."

Unable to comprehend or accept such sudden, final news, I asked: "How bad is it? What chance is there for her?"

The doctor replied, "It is the worst possible case of tetanus poisoning, for she had an incubation period of less than a week and has the full force of the poisoning. There is no chance that she can live; she will be dead before night. There is nothing we can do for her but to put her under sedation so her death will be as painless as possible."

I replied, "If she is to die anyway, then I will take her home and let her die with her family."

"The law of this state forbids us to release a person we know is dying," the doctor said, "We must keep her here, and will do the best we can to make her dying easy."

With hearts of lead my wife and I returned to the place where we were staying. Naturally we prayed all the way back. I went immediately to my room and fell to my knees in prayer and weeping. I told the Lord that I would not eat or drink again until I heard from Him concerning my precious daughter.

Sharon did not die that day, nor the next; in fact three days passed with the doctors wondering how she remained alive. Each day they assured me she could not live until night, and each night they assured me she could not survive until the day. Because of her desperate condition we were not allowed to stay in the room with her. Despite her deep sedation the slightest sound threw her into violent spasms. A private nurse was by her bedside at all times to help make her dying easy.

After three days I was very weak from my fast, sorrow of heart and loss of sleep. I lay quietly on a couch while my wife read aloud from the Scriptures. As she was reading from John 15 she came to verse 7: "If ye abide in me, and my words abide in you, ye shall ask what ye will, and it shall be done unto you." Something wonderful happened to me at the sound of those words, and a faith took hold of my heart that was not of my own doing. God touched me with faith as surely as if I heard Jesus Himself say those wonderful words. In that brilliant moment I knew that Sharon would be healed and restored to her family. I sat upright and exclaimed:

"Darling, that message is for us. It is as clear as if it had said, 'Dear Charles and Edna,' and was signed 'God.' "

From that day forward I had no doubt, no anxiety, no fear, and no dread. I knew that she would live, that she would be raised up by the healing power of God. I only waited patiently until the work of God should be complete. No dire warnings and no temporary emergencies could shake the tenacity of that faith. God could have raised her up immediately, and He very often does heal in that very way, but He allowed me to have full proof of that manifestion of faith by letting it be tested by the doubts of doctors and the passing of dark days.

On a wonderful day shortly afterward I had the joyful experience of carrying my daughter from the hospital, healed and made whole by the power of God. Sharon is a grown lady now, the mother of her own family, happy in the service of the Lord, enjoying the blessings of strength and health.

Just last summer I witnessed a manifestation of faith of this sort in a fellow minister. His daughter became ill and medical diagnosis showed her to have leukemia. We were in a camp meeting at the time and many persons were praying for the daughter's healing. On the day following the dreaded diagnosis, when the outcome was very uncertain, the father told me, "While I was praying last night I suddenly knew that she will be all right. I don't know why, but I know that she will be healed and restored to us."

The daughter was healed, miraculously, wonderfully and came to the meeting before it closed. It was she who experienced the miracle of healing, but it was the father who experienced the gift of faith.

This kind of faith does not come every day, for it is not needed every day. It is Divine, miraculous, and usually intercessory. Many times the gift of faith is for our own healing and our own circumstances, but more often it comes to a person on behalf of another when that person is unable to have faith for himself (Matthew 17:20, 21; James 5:15).

5. *GIFTS OF HEALING*

In our day healing is obviously the most desired, most sought after and most coveted spiritual gift of all. This has not always been so, for the Corinthian church seemed to be particularly taken with the gift of tongues. In the early days of the Pentecostal movement it was the same with us, and the Pentecostal people were frequently known as "the tongues people." That circumstance has changed now, and the gifts of healing seem to be in greatest prominence.

Notice that this is listed in the plural—"gifts of healing"—the only plural listing among the Gifts. This is obviously due to the fact that there are so many kinds of diseases, maladies and sicknesses that many forms of healing are required for their cure. Modern understanding of the complex nature of man, his body, and his mind has increased our understanding of the many ways in which he may be sick. I suppose there is no catalog that lists all the illnesses among men. Some are physical, some are emotional and some are mental; some are temporary and some are permanent; some are real and some are imaginary; some are common and some are rare—but all indicate a degree of distress in the human race.

Healing was one of the primary purposes of the ministry of Christ, and the record of His healings is almost as extensive as that of His preaching. It is also noteworthy that when Jesus sent His twelve disciples out He empowered them to cast out devils and "heal *all manner* of sickness and *all manner* of disease" (Matthew 10:1). The repetition of the words "all manner" emphasizes that even in Bible times there was a recognition of the great multiplicity of kinds of sickness. The Gospels and the book of Acts are so replete with accounts of healing that it would be useless to try to recount them. No scriptural fact is more thoroughly established than the fact of Divine healing.

But healing did not stop with the apostles. It is the promise of the Lord that healing is to be a prominent part of the church's spiritual service. From the beginning of the Pentecostal Movement Divine healing has been associated with the baptism of the Holy Ghost. In every account of early outpourings that I have read I have noted that miraculous healings also took place. This is one of the distinctives of the Pentecostal Movement. Men and women are alive today who once were dying with cancer, tuberculosis and other deadly diseases.

When I was a young pastor in Missouri it was discovered that my wife had a tumor of the uterus. The physician attending her called me to his office and explained carefully that surgery would be required. He also showed me photographs to impress me with the seriousness of her condition. The tumor had been discovered and confirmed during the birth of our eldest daughter, and the fact that both mother and child were alive was miracle enough. I should not hope for another.

As I have done throughout my Christian life, I began to fast for God to manifest Himself in our time of distress. After about two days I felt assurance that God had heard our prayers and healed my wife. Beforehand the large tumor had been clearly evident. After her healing there was no further indication that it had ever existed.

A minister friend and his wife, Gordon and Lulu Watson, both saints of much prayer and great faith, visited us and we four gave ourselves to prayer for healing. While we were praying I interrupted the others and said, "I feel that my praying this way is a lack of faith; God has already given me assurance that my wife is healed."

Our dear sainted friend said, "Then let us praise Him for what He has done." We then praised God for the work of healing that had been done.

My wife went immediately to the clinic for an examination. The physician was very apologetic when he said, "Mrs. Conn, I can't explain what has happened, but there is no sign of a tumor anymore." She explained joyfully how God had healed her by His power.

This was the healing of an organic illness; and physicians have been bewildered by many other such miraculous healings. Go into any Pentecostal congregation and ask those who have been Divinely healed to raise their hands, and you will see a forest of uplifted hands in testimony to the healing power of God.

The agencies of healing are many. Jesus healed by putting spittle on a blind man's eyes (John 9:6, 7); the sick were healed when even the shadow of Simon Peter passed over them (Acts 5:15); handkerchiefs or cloths were sent out

GIFTS OF THE SPIRIT 129

from Paul, and those who received them were healed of their diseases, or freed from demon possession (Acts 19:11, 12). Followers of Christ are instructed to use two principal agencies in prayer for the sick. One of these is anointing with oil. It is said that the disciples "cast out many devils, and anointed with oil many that were sick, and healed them" (Mark 6:13). James 5:14 says: "Is any sick among you? let him call for the elders of the church; and let them pray over him, anointing him with oil in the name of the Lord."

The second agency for spiritual healing is the laying on of hands. "They shall lay hands on the sick, and they shall recover" (Mark 16:18). There is nothing to indicate that this form of healing is necessarily a manifestation of the gifts of healing. It seems instead to be simply a regular part of Christian worship and service. The gift of healing is something much more; it is a supernatural, frequently instantaneous, healing of an illness that could not be cured naturally. Nothing less than the power of the Holy Spirit could effect such miracles.

6. THE WORKING OF MIRACLES

This brings us to a consideration of the third operative gift—the working of miracles. In a rather comprehensive study of the Gifts of the Spirit, Harold Horton defines a miracle in this way:

> A miracle, therefore, is a supernatural intervention in the ordinary course of nature; a temporary suspension of the accustomed order; an interruption of the system of nature as we know it. The Gift of the Working of Miracles operates by the energy or dynamic force of the Spirit in reversals or suspensions of natural laws. A miracle is a sovereign act of the Spirit of God irrespective of laws or systems. A miracle does not, as some cynical unbelievers say, demand the existence of an undiscovered law to explain it. A miracle has no explanation other than the sovereign power of the Lord. God

is not bound by His own laws. God acts as He will either within or outside of what we understand to be laws, whether natural or supernatural. So to speak of God as though He were circumscribed by the laws of His own making is to reduce Him to the creature plane and impair the very essence of His eternal attributes. When in a sudden and sovereign act God steps outside the circle by which His creatures or creation are boundaried we call it a miracle. And so does God in the Scriptures[16]

In the four accounts of Christ's life we have the record of many miracles. He changed water into wine at the marriage in Cana of Galilee; He stilled a raging storm; He walked upon the surface of the Sea of Galilee; He produced sufficient food to feed five thousand on one occasion and four thousand on another; He disappeared from among those who intended to do Him bodily harm; He replaced an ear that had been severed from a man's head; and He performed many other miraculous works. He promised His disciples that if they had sufficient faith they would be able to move mountains (Matthew 17:20). It is interesting that Jesus used this statement in connection with the disciples' effort to cast the devil out of a man. He concluded His statement about the possible moving a mountain by saying, "Howbeit this kind goeth not out but by prayer and fasting" (Matthew 17:21). In this way He equated the casting out of devils with the working of miracles. This is also in agreement with many other sections of Scripture where healings and the casting out of devils occurred side by side but were regarded as different operations. Below are a few such references:

"When the even was come, they brought unto him many that were possessed with devils: and he cast out the spirits with his word, and healed all that were sick" (Matthew 8:16).

"And his fame went throughout all Syria: and they brought unto him all sick people that were taken with divers diseases and torments, and those which were possesed with devils, and those which were lunatick, and those that had the palsy; and he healed them" (Matthew 4:24).

"And at even, when the sun did set, they brought unto him all that were diseased, and them that were possessed with devils. And he healed many that were sick of divers diseases, and cast out many devils; and suffered not the devils to speak, because they knew him" (Mark 1:32, 34).

"And he said unto them, Go ye, and tell that fox, Behold, I cast out devils, and I do cures to day and to morrow, and the third day I shall be perfected" (Luke 13:32).

In the book of Acts there are also numerous accounts of miracles performed by the apostles. Peter's release from prison through the intervention of an angel was such a miracle; the release of Paul and Silas from prison in Philippi; and Paul's immunity to snakebite on Melita were all supernatural miracles. On at least two occasions the apostles raised the dead to life. Peter raised up Dorcas (Acts 9:40, 41) and Paul raised up Eutychus (Acts 20:9, 10).

It is noteworthy that in the book of Acts we find the same parallel of working miracles and casting out devils that we found in Christ's statement to His disciples. Note these two accounts regarding Philip and Paul.

"And the people with one accord gave heed unto those things which Philip spake, hearing and seeing the *miracles* which he did. For *unclean spirits,* crying with loud voice, came out of many that were possessed with them: and many taken with palsies, and that were lame, were healed" (Acts 8: 6, 7).

"And God wrought special *miracles* by the hands of Paul: So that from his body were brought unto the sick handkerchiefs or aprons, and the *diseases departed* from them, and the *evil spirits* went out of them" (Acts 19:11, 12).

We must conclude that the casting out of devils is the most prominent form of working a miracle. Other miracles are certainly possible, but they have not been prevalent in either the record of the apostles or the Pentecostal history. But of the casting out of devils there is a long record of deliverance and liberation.

THE GIFTS OF INSPIRATION

The final three manifestations involve the speech of the individual. I call them "gifts of inspiration" because the inspiration of the Spirit is required in each of them. These gifts are always the first to be associated with the Holy Ghost Baptism, and they have become conspicuous distinctives of the Pentecostal Revival. Because they involve the human voice they are subject to much abuse and occasional disorder. This may relate to the unruly nature of the human tongue, concerning which James said:

> Even so the tongue is a little member, and boasteth great things. Behold, how great a matter a little fire kindleth! And the tongue is a fire, a world of iniquity: so is the tongue among our members, that it defileth the whole body, and setteth on fire the course of nature; and it is set on fire of hell. But the tongue can no man tame; it is an unruly evil, full of deadly poison (James 3:5, 6, 8).

Because of this harmful nature of the carnal tongue, great emphasis is placed upon bringing our words under the control of the Holy Spirit.

The gifts of inspiration are among the most beautiful manifestations of the Holy Spirit in the church today. They occur when the Spirit moves upon an individual to give ecstatic admonition or comfort to the congregation. The manifestations may be in a human language, but unknown to the worshipers (tongues), or in an ecstatic language unknown to anyone (unknown tongues), or in the native language of the worshipers (prophecy). However the message comes it must be orderly and in full agreement with the Word of God. When He who inspired the Scriptures speaks to the church today it will be in accord with what is written. There is always concord between the written and spoken words of the Spirit.

7. PROPHECY

The gift of prophecy and the office of a prophet (the Ministry Gifts) are not the same thing: only the names are similar. (A prophet in the New Testament was one who regularly performed prophetic ministries in the church. The four daughters to Philip were prophetesses, and Agabus was called a prophet [Acts 21:8-10]. This apparently refers to their frequent or accustomed prophecies in the church.)

Manifestations of prophecy as a gift of the Spirit are no more confined to a minister-prophet than any other gifts would be. This gift-prophecy is as miraculous, spontaneous and Spirit-motivated as are the word of wisdom, healing, or speaking in tongues. Like all the other gifts, prophecy occurs at a time when it is needed for the edification of the body of Christ.

Paul had very much to say about prophecy in 1 Corinthians 14. He encouraged the Corinthians to "follow after charity, and desire spiritual gifts, but rather that ye may prophesy. But he that prophesieth speaketh unto men to edification, and exhortation, and comfort. He that speaketh in an unknown tongue edifieth himself; but he that prophesieth edifieth the church. I would that ye all spake with tongues, but rather that ye prophesied: for greater is he that prophesieth than he that speaketh with tongues, except he interpret, that the church may receive edifying" (1 Corinthians 14:1, 3, 4, 5).

It should be observed that Paul contrasted prophecy with tongues and interpretation. The meaning is quite clear that prophecy achieves alone what tongues and interpretation achieve together.

Prophecy, as a gift of the Spirit, is not foretelling the future. Naturally foretelling future events can be an aspect of any prophecy, but it is never the primary meaning of it. A study of the prophecies of the Bible will reveal that only a small part deals with the future, while the greater part deals with needs of the present.

Some people imagine that prophecy is in reality the function of preaching, and whenever a man stands to preach the Christian message he is being used with the gift of prophecy. The giving forth of prophecy may in many ways resemble ordinary preaching, but it is something very different. I have been a preacher of God's Word for the past thirty-five years, about two-thirds of my life, and have preached under all circumstances. I have preached when the anointing upon me has been great and overpowering; I have preached with good anointing; and I have preached with great difficulty when there was little evidence of anointing. No, the gift of prophecy is a manifestation of greater distinction than the normal course of preaching the Word.

I have seen this gift operate many times in the church. It is beautiful, powerful and exceedingly effective. The same as a person who speaks with other tongues, the one who gives forth prophecy is enrapt in the Spirit and speaks in his own language a message direct from the heart of God. The person so used is a vessel in God's hands, used for the giving of an ecstatic message, penetrating and understanding, for the upbuilding of the body of Christ.

I recall a time when I was deeply burdened about conditions in the church where I was pastor and I spent a Sunday afternoon in the churchhouse alone praying and seeking God on behalf of the congregation. My heart seemed as if it would burst with compassion and concern for the little flock God had placed in my trust. During the course of the service that night, the Spirit of God was great upon me, not with external emotion but with the deepest feeling of solemnity and burden. As I approached the pulpit for my sermon the Spirit moved upon me so that all my pent-up care and concern burst forth. Prophetic utterance gushed forth as if a dam had broken, releasing the swollen stream of spiritual concern behind it. For twenty or thirty minutes the message streamed forth, but it was God's message and not my own. I was nothing more than a yielded vessel He was using for His purpose. Naturally I was aware of what I was saying and I probably could have ceased if I had determined to do so (1 Corinthians 14:32), but the message was Spirit-inspired and Spirit-borne. This has happened to me many times since then, and it is always very much the same.

Let me repeat that the gift of prophecy is ecstatic utterance that "speaketh unto men to edification, and exhortation, and comfort" (1 Corinthians 14:3). The purpose of the gift is clearly stated, and it will always bring edification, exhortation and comfort to the body of Christ. It is a miracle of God given at the moment to meet the pressing need of God's people. When it works properly in the church it is one of the most beautiful of all the manifestations of the Spirit.

8. DIVERS KINDS OF TONGUES

The gift of the Spirit that has gained the greatest attention is the gift of tongues. Because of this manifestation Pentecostal people have frequently been called "tongues people." As unfair and unfortunate as this is, it is understandable. Such gifts as the word of wisdom, the word of knowledge, the discerning of spirits and faith work quietly in the heart and mind of the individual. There is rarely any public awareness of them. The gifts of healing and the working of miracles are manifestly beneficial, because any effort to relieve suffering and foster healing can only be looked on as something commendable. Even prophecy may be tolerated, even though not appreciated, as understandable and impassioned exhortation. It is different with tongues, for unbelievers are unable to understand what is said and often fail to see its purposes and benefits. Speaking with other tongues has become the chief distinction of the Pentecostal movement, as well as its greatest stigma.

There are two kinds of tongues that occur in Scripture. The first is related to the outpouring of the Holy Ghost, which was always attended by conspicuous spiritual manifestations, especially that of speaking with unknown tongues, that is, languages. This phenomenon was the consistent evidence that the Holy Spirit had come into the hearts of men. This occurred on the Day of Pentecost when the disciples received the Holy Ghost (Acts 2:4). It happened in the house of Cornelius when they received the Holy Ghost (Acts 10:46). It happened in Ephesus when the disciples in that city received the Holy Ghost (Acts 19:6). Although it is not specifically stated in the English text, the original Greek shows plainly that those who received the Holy Ghost in Samaria also spoke in tongues (Acts 8:14-18). This consistency must not be ignored.

An important observation should be made at this point. Speaking in tongues upon receiving the Holy Spirit is not an exercise of the gift of tongues. It is an initial proof or evidence that the believer has been baptized in the Holy Spirit. Many other evidences of the Spirit's presence are observed later, such as spiritual dedication, and power, consistent spiritual boldness, increased effectiveness in the Lord's service, absorption in spiritual things, and progress toward Christian maturity. These evidences of the Spirit's presence require the passing of time, but speaking with tongues occurs immediately and gives witness that the Spirit has come. We therefore refer to this occasion of speaking with tongues as the initial evidence of the Spirit Baptism.

If speaking with tongues at the time of being baptized with the Spirit were an exercise of the Gift of the Spirit, then there would surely be frequent manifestations of the other eight gifts as well. There is no indication that persons receiving the Holy Ghost ever healed the sick, cast out devils, discerned evil spirits or otherwise manifested a gift of the Spirit at the time of their Baptism. There were three accompanying spiritual phenomena on the Day of Pentecost: the sound of a rushing mighty wind, the appearance of cloven tongues like as of fire, and speaking with tongues. Of the three spiritual phenomena that occurred on Pentecost, only the speaking with tongues continued in later outpourings recorded in the Book of Acts. The wind and the fire were obviously one-time manifestations. From scriptural reference and historical experience it becomes clear to us that speaking with tongues is the one immediate indication —or initial evidence—that believers have received the baptism of the Holy Spirit.

The gift of tongues is a continuing part of Christian service, set in the church for the edifying of the body of Christ and Christian witness. The Corinthian Christians had obviously become enamored of the sensational and spectacular gift of tongues and had exalted it above the other gifts, thereby abusing it. Paul wrote extensively to the Corinthians to correct their abuses of the gift of tongues. Those who use 1 Corinthians 14 to disprove the validity of tongues miss the point altogether. Paul endeavored to correct the abuses but was very careful that his admonitions not discourage the proper use of tongues.

> "I thank my God, I speak with tongues more than ye all:
> Wherefore tongues are for a sign, not to them that believe,
> but to them that believe not. . . . Wherefore, brethren, covet
> to prophesy, and forbid not to speak with tongues" (1 Co-
> rinthians 14:18, 22, 39).

The parallel of tongues and prophecy shows that both manifestations are generally for the same purpose: edification, exhortation and comfort (1 Corinthians 14:3). Although other purposes have been served by the exercise of tongues, the principal purpose seems to be the edification of the individual believer and the congregation of the Lord.

The gift is noted as "divers kinds of tongues" (1 Corinthians 12:10), which signifies a diversity in the kinds of tongues spoken and in the purposes of the manifestation. The word "tongues" itself means "languages." Frequently Spirit-filled believers speak in languages they have never learned, but are common and recognizable human languages. I have heard numbers of testimonies of those who were won to Christ through such witness of the Spirit. Frequently persons have come to me following worship services to relate that their native language is German, Russian, Italian or some other, and that a message in tongues during the worship service was in that language.

Then there is a speaking in ecstacy that is not the language of anyone on earth. Paul refers to the tongues of men and of angels (1 Corinthians 13:1), which is probably a reference to this ecstatic utterance. This is also done for the edification of the congregation. As with all the other gifts, speaking with tongues is a spontaneous spiritual manifestation, miraculously given by the Holy Ghost at a time when it is needed and in accordance with His will.

OTHER FORMS OF THE GIFT

The first time I witnessed devotional singing in tongues, which is intimated in 1 Corinthians 14:15, was during my

freshman year in college. The student body was in prayer
during a chapel service when a young lady began to sing in
tongues. She sang alone, softly and beautifully, for a few
moments and then another girl joined her, then another,
and still another. Soon six or seven persons were singing
together in tongues, with the same words and the same
melody, from various parts of the auditorium. There was
no possibility of collusion however: at that time the school
term had just begun and the students were from all parts
of the United States, in no way acquainted with one another. The girl who first began to sing has for more than
thirty years been my wife and constant companion, and I
know the life of dedication and devotion that backs this
manifestation. On many occasions since that time the Spirit
has moved upon her in the same way.

Far more frequently the Spirit is manifested by praying
in tongues, to which Paul makes specific reference (1 Corinthians 14:2, 14, 15). Often in prayer the Spirit-filled
supplicant will be moved upon by a manifestation of tongues
as the Holy Spirit intercedes for him. Paul said; "Likewise
the Spirit also helpeth our infirmities: for we know not
what we should pray for as we ought: but the Spirit itself
maketh intercession for us with groanings which cannot be
uttered" (Romans 8:26).

Critics of the exercise of tongues have sometimes suggested, or even accused, that those who speak in tongues do
so to draw attention to themselves, that they manifest the
gift only in the company of others. This is totally false.
Having been a participant and observer of the Pentecostal
Movement for more than three decades, I know that the
gift is manifested in times of private prayer and devotion
fully as often, and possibly more often, than in public worship. This agrees with what Paul said in 1 Corinthians 14:
19: "Yet in the church I had rather speak five words with

140   A BALANCED CHURCH

my understanding, that by my voice I might teach others also, than ten thousand words in an unknown tongue." The practice of speaking in tongues during prayer is in accord with the fact that "he that speaketh in an unknown tongue speaketh not unto men, but unto God" (1 Corinthians 14:2).

9. INTERPRETATION OF TONGUES

The last of the gifts of inspiration—and the last of all nine gifts—is the interpretation of tongues. By its very name it is seen that this gift operates only in conjunction with the gift of tongues. No other gift is mentioned specifically as being attendant to another gift. This means that it can never work alone, for its manifestation is to explain another gift. Another interesting observation about the interpretation of tongues is that it is the only gift without scriptural reference to its manifestation. There are records of how all the other eight gifts were used among the apostles, but there is no specific mention of tongues being interpreted. That is not necessary, however, for the meaning and purpose of the gift are obvious.

Interpretation is an explanation of something unknown or not understood. When someone speaks in tongues the message is unknown to the congregation unless someone interprets it for them. It is for this reason that Paul said, "Let him that speaketh in an unknown tongue pray that he may interpret" (1 Corinthians 14:13). It is emphasized throughout Paul's discourse that when interpretation does not accompany tongues, the understanding is lost. The individual who speaks in tongues may be edified (v. 4) but the congregation is blessed with understanding only when the interpretation comes. The one who speaks in tongues should pray for the interpretation. The one who speaks in tongues is frequently used for the interpretation, but not always. Just as often the interpretation of a message will be manifested through another worshipper. But if there is no interpretation the one who speaks in tongues is responsible to pray for it (14:13).

The manifestation of tongues and the accompanying interpretation is a beautiful and powerful experience in Christian worship. At great camp meetings and assemblies where thousands of people are in attendance it is a thrilling thing to hear one person speak out in tongues while thousands sit in silence. When the message is complete the Spirit moves upon another worshipper who distinctly and in order gives the interpretation of what has been said. The interpreter speaks in the same ecstacy as the one who spoke with tongues. The message is almost always one of edification, exhortation and comfort. There are also times when the message is one of admonition or rebuke.

INTERPRETATION AND TRANSLATION

We need to know what interpretation is. Some are disturbed when the message in tongues and the interpretation do not agree in length. In most instances, tongues and the interpretation will be of the same duration, from a brief utterance to a lengthy oration. There are other times that the message in tongues will be of rather long extent and the interpretation will be very brief. At still other times the manifestation of tongues may be short and the interpretation will be lengthy. This disturbs some listeners who feel that they should always agree in extent. The interpretation of tongues, however, is exactly that—an *interpretation* rather than a translation. In a translation, which is generally a word-for-word transmission from one language to another, this would be true, but in interpretation it is not always so. It is an interpreting in a known language what has just been said in an unknown language. The purpose of both translation and interpretation is communication and understanding.

In the course of my ministry I have preached in about seventy countries, and my preaching has been translated into many languages. Generally what I say in English and what is translated into another language correspond closely in duration, but there are occasions when I make a brief statement that requires a great deal of interpretation or explanation by the interpreter. Problems, of national customs, native expressions and figures of speech have a great deal to do with this.

In a limited way these problems of natural interpretation also affect spiritual interpretation. Not nearly as much, however, for in tongues and interpretation the Holy Spirit is the agency for both utterances. It does not matter a great deal, because the entire function of tongues and interpretation is to achieve the same result as prophecy: edification, exhortation and comfort.

Now we have looked at the nine typical Gifts of the Spirit listed in 1 Corinthians 12:8-10. Unlike the Fruit, which is unified, the Gifts are diverse. They do agree, however, and work together for one purpose, administered by the same Spirit. To be a balanced church we must have all nine working harmoniously in our services, in our labor, and in our lives. If we give disproportionate emphasis to any one of the gifts we will be erratic and out of balance, certain to veer off the course God intends for us. These are manifestations of the power that has been given us to do the work of Jesus Christ, and when they work regularly and orderly among us we will be able to do what He has called us to do.

PART FOUR

THE MINISTRY GIFTS

*And he gave some, apostles; and some, prophets;
and some, evangelists; and some, pastors and teachers; for the perfecting of the saints, for the work
of the ministry, for the edifying of the body of
Christ (Ephesians 4:11, 12).*

*And God hath set some in the church, first apos-
tles, secondarily prophets, thirdly teachers, after that
miracles, then gifts of healings, helps, governments,
diversities of tongues (1 Corinthians 12:28).*

4

THE MINISTRY GIFTS

WHY GOD USES MEN

The third element Christ has given the church is Christian ministry. Having endowed His people with the fruit of holiness and the power of the Spirit, He completed His work by giving direction, order and guidance through anointed men. God could have proclaimed His kingdom on earth without the agency of the church and the ministry of men, but it would not have been as effective. He has manifestly chosen the most effective way of declaring His will to mankind.

God could have written His message in stars across the sky so men could read it each time they look upward. He could have caused His Word to boom audibly around the world so none could escape hearing it, or He could have showered it on tables like manna from heaven. But God chose a more effective way.

God could have used angels as His ministers, and He did that in a few instances (Genesis 19). But He has chosen men to minister to men because no angel could ever under-

145

stand human needs. What does an angel know about the struggle against sin, or about pressing financial obligations, or the worry about willful children, or the pains of infirmity, or about any of the trials that make all men brethren? So God chose men to be His ministers, so that they might speak to other men of common needs, common responsibilities and common possibilities.

When I was first called into the ministry I wrote the following lines:

> What need has God of angels bold
> Or starlit words across the sky?
> He calls for men to preach His Word
> To other men about to die. ¯

Although it is not great poetry, this does express the truth of God's design for the proclamation of His Word.

When Jesus was on earth He gathered many disciples, men whom He taught the principles of the kingdom of God. From among the multitude of His disciples, Jesus chose twelve to be apostles (Luke 6:13), which twelve became the foundation of the Christian ministry. Many others were chosen to join them in the ministry of the Word.

THE DIVINE CALLING

When Jesus was on earth He personally called men into kingdom service. He said to Peter and Andrew, "Follow me, and I will make you fishers of men" (Matthew 4:19); He said to Philip, "Follow me" (John 1:43); and to Nathaniel, "Hereafter ye shall see heaven open, and the angels of God ascending and descending upon the Son of man" (John 1:51); and to Matthew He also said, "Follow me" (Matthew 9:9). In similar fashion Jesus called the twelve apostles into His service. Matthew 10:1 says that "When he had called unto him his twelve disciples, he gave them power against unclean spirits, to cast them out, and to heal all manner of sickness and all manner of disease." The commission He gave the Twelve is recorded in some detail in Matthew 10:1-42.

Not all of those who came into contact with Jesus and were partakers of His grace were called into Divine service. When He cast the devils out of a man called Legion in the country of the Gadarenes, the man desired to follow Jesus and become one of His disciples. Instead, Jesus told him to "return to thine own house" (Luke 8:39).

The Divine calling of Christ continued through the book of Acts. Concerning Saul of Tarsus He said, "He is a chosen vessel unto me, to bear my name before the Gentiles, and kings, and the children of Israel: For I will shew him how great things he must suffer for my name's sake" (Acts 9:15, 16). In later reference to Barnabas and Saul, it is recorded that "the Holy Ghost said, Separate me Barnabas and Saul for the work whereunto I have called them" (Acts 13:2). Paul himself gave an eloquent testimony of his calling during his defense before King Agrippa (Acts 26:13-18).

In the early days of the church strong emphasis was placed upon a Divine calling into the vocation of the gospel (Romans 11:29; 2 Timothy 1:6-11). With the spiritual calling there came special anointing and supernatural gifts that enabled the called person to do the work to which he was appointed. Through the passing of centuries man's awareness of this calling became neglected, overlooked and replaced by other motivations. The time came when men went into ministerial careers for benign and altruistic reasons, but without any sense of having been called of God to do so. They had admirable desires to benefit mankind, but the ministry became to them a career, a profession, a job—instead of a calling.

There have always been men who have felt a Divine

calling, but they have been greatly outnumbered by those who know too little of the Spirit of God. As the Gadarene would have done, they go forth without having been called. More tragic still, they regard the ministry a job, like the hireling of John 10:12, 13, and work without the heart of a shepherd.

Christ intends His church to have a Divinely called ministry, spiritually empowered, and totally dedicated to His service. Quite naturally those who are called must equip themselves with the finest training and most thorough preparation possible for them. In fact, the calling of God assumes such periods of preparation before actually launching into the ministry. Following the initial call of the apostles there was a training period of about three years when they worked with the Lord. Paul's full-time ministry began about twelve years after his conversion and call, during which time the apostle-to-be remained in his home city of Tarsus (Acts 11:25, 26).

One of the greatest blessings of the Pentecostal Revival in this century has been its emphasis upon the callings of God and the supernatural gifts that accompany those callings. As it was in the days of the prophets and the apostles, men have been, and still are, called from humble backgrounds, unheralded and unpromising, to become the most capable ministers and do the most extraordinary works. Donald Gee, an early Pentecostal leader whom I learned to know well and love much before his recent death, once said:

> We believe the Pentecostal Movement will absolutely fail in obedience to the heavenly vision God placed before it, if it goes back to dependence upon purely natural gifts for the work of the ministry; never mind how deeply people may be consecrated, or how efficiently they may be educated in Bible schools or elsewhere. The holding steadily before us of the visions of the supernatural gifts of the Spirit, and their resultant ministry-gifts, is of vital importance.[17]

THREEFOLD PURPOSE OF THE MINISTRY

As with the Fruit of the Spirit and the Gifts of the Spirit, the Ministry Gifts have a clear pattern that fits with and completes the plan of the church. Since the days of the apostles there have been numerous aspects and expressions of Christian ministry, but in one way or another they serve the threefold purpose of evangelism, watchcare and administration. The ministry is ordained to lead in the rescue of lost souls, the nurture and preservation of those who are rescued, and in directing the work of rescue and conservation. This purpose is diagramed as follows:

Evangelism. Every work of the ministry fulfills one of these three purposes. The initial need of the ministry was to evangelize the world, and the tremendous work of evangelism remains a great responsibility of the church. At no time has the work of evangelism been completed, and it is as urgently needed today as it was in the days of the apostles. Apostles and evangelists are those ministers primarily anointed for the vital work of winning the world to the kingdom of God.

Watchcare. The ministry of watchcare is necessary for the preservation and upbuilding of that which has been won to Christ through evangelism. For this purpose God anoints prophets, pastors and teachers. We shall later examine more carefully the purpose and responsibility of these ministry gifts.

Administration. A third necessity for church work is that of administration and guidance, which 1 Corinthians 12:28 refers to as "governments." The purpose of administration is to give order, direction, unity and regulation to the body of Christ. It is a mistaken notion that administration constricts and confines the body of Christ. It increases effectiveness in the work of the church.

If we should neglect any function of the ministry we would run into the dangers of ineffectiveness, overlapping and fanaticism. On the other hand if we emphasize the ministry, especially its church organization, beyond that which is intended in Scripture, we run into a danger of establishing a powerless hierarchy. It would be a doleful thing to live in a church that emphasizes the Fruit but has become ineffective through the absence of the Gifts. It would be equally tragic to live in a church that emphasizes the Gifts but has become fanatic through deemphasis of the Fruit or wanton through a despising of government (2 Peter 2:10). It would be even more oppressive to live in a church that has developed strong organization without the spiritual presence of the Fruit or the power of the Gifts. The three are to work together in harmony to do the kingdom work of God.

THE FIVE MINISTRY GIFTS

For its functions of evangelism, watchcare, and administration, the Lord has given the church five particular Ministry Gifts. These are listed in Ephesians 4:11, 12: "And he gave some, apostles; and some, prophets; and some, evangelists: and some. pastors and teachers: for the perfecting of the saints, for the work of the ministry, for the edifying of the body of Christ." Paul made an additional reference to the gifts in 1 Corinthians 12:28: "And God hath set some in the church, first apostles, secondarily prophets, thirdly teachers, after that miracles, then gifts of healings, helps, governments, diversities of tongues." In the statement to the Corinthians Paul intermixed the Ministry Gifts with the Gifts of the Spirit, which is rather common in Scripture. The very fact that the Fruit of the Spirit, the Gifts of the Spirit, and the Ministry Gifts are frequently intermixed in scriptural listings proves the assumption that all three elements are expected to work harmoniously in the body of Christ.

Just as there is interlinking of the Fruit and overlapping of the Gifts, there is an overlapping of the Ministry Gifts. A successful evangelist must have times when he is a prophet or a pastor or teacher. A pastor likewise must frequently do the work of an evangelist or a prophet. None of the Ministry Gifts lives alone in a cubicle without extending in both directions to join other gifts. Each gift is manifested in the manner which God most frequently directs and uses His minister.

The Bible does not give us precise directions regarding church structure. There are many references to various aspects of the ministry, such as bishop (1 Timothy 3:1-7); deacons (1 Timothy 3:8-13); presbyters (1 Timothy 4:14), and elders (2 John 1), but there is no indication that these offices were in addition to the Ministry Gifts already mentioned. They were apparently differing aspects of the same ministry. At a later point we will look at some of these distinctive services.

For the time being, we will look at the Ephesian list of Ministry Gifts—apostles, prophets, evangelists, pastors and teachers.

1. *APOSTLES*

The first order of the ministry in the New Testament is that of apostles. The term "apostle" means "a messenger" or "one who is sent," seen in the words of Jesus, "as my Father hath sent me, even so send I you" (John 20:21). An apostle is one who was sent by the Lord to be His special emissary and to do a special work. There were three qualifying requirements for the apostles, and only by meeting the three could anyone qualify for apostleship. First of all, an apostle's work must be based upon the work of Jesus Christ, that is, apostolic work must be a direct extension of Christ's ministry. Note that Jesus - Himself was called an apostle in Hebrews 3:1: "Wherefore, holy brethren, partakers of the heavenly calling, consider the Apostle and High Priest of our profession, Christ Jesus."

A second qualification was that an apostle must have personally seen the Lord. This condition was spelled out by the original apostles as they sought a replacement for Judas Iscariot (Acts 1:22). We may be sure that they did not impose this qualification arbitrarily; it must have been a well-established qualification known and understood by everyone. Paul was aware of that requirement even though he had not been one of the original Twelve, for he defended his apostleship by specifically stating that he had seen the Lord (1 Corinthians 15:7-9). The only way he had seen Jesus was by vision on the Damascus road at the time of his conversion.

The requirement that an apostle must have seen the Lord affirms that the apostolic work was a direct continuation of the Lord's ministry. The purpose for this was that those called apostles could give firsthand witness to the resurrection of Christ. They had seen Him alive after His crucifixion and personally knew that He had overcome death.

A third qualification for apostleship was the laying of an original foundation (Ephesians 2:20). Once again, Paul defended his apostleship by declaring that he had done foundation work in his service to Christ. "Yea, so have I strived to preach the gospel, not where Christ was named, lest I should build upon another man's foundation" (Romans 15:20). "According to the grace of God which is given unto me, as a wise masterbuilder, I have laid the foundation, and another buildeth thereon. But let every man take heed how he buildeth thereupon" (1 Corinthians 3:10). Paul called the Corinthian church his proof of legitimacy as an apostle. "If I be not an apostle unto others, yet doubtless I am to you: for the seal of mine apostleship are ye in the Lord" (1 Corinthians 9:2).

How many apostles were there in the New Testament? We will never know, but there were several mentioned by name. First of all, there were the original Twelve, and then Matthias was chosen to replace Judas. Paul was the most prominent apostle who did not serve with Jesus during His lifetime. Some felt that Paul was not a legitimate apostle for that very reason but he defended his apostleship strongly, "For in nothing am I behind the very chiefest apostles, though I be nothing" (2 Corinthians 12:11). Barnabas is mentioned along with Paul as being an apostle (Acts 14:14); Paul's kinsmen, Andronicus and Junia, are referred to as apostles in Romans 16:7. This brings to quite a list those who were specifically known as apostles. Moreover, the fact that false apostles were condemned (2 Corinthians 11:13) suggests that there were a considerable number of apostles at that time.

Occasionally we hear of apostles in this century. No one can deny that this is a possibility, for it was possible with Paul; but it is most uncommon, if not altogether unlikely. The office of apostle is one of the Ministry Gifts set in the church, so we should not say that the apostleship could not exist today. My only observation is that Christ is consistent, and the requirements of apostolic times would still prevail today. This means that a person would have to have a personal revelation of the Lord Jesus Christ before he could be regarded as an apostle. He would have to do a primary work, the laying of a foundation where no one had ever built before. While these things are possible they are not likely to be frequent or common. Primitive missionary work is about the only way that it could really be conceivable. By and large the apostolic work was completed in apostolic times.

2. PROPHETS

Second of the orders of Christian ministry is that of prophet. This is the only ministerial order that has a directly-related gift of the Spirit, that of prophecy. The distinction seems to be that the gift of prophecy is a spiritual inspiration that might happen to any believer in time of need. The office of the prophet was as continuing as the office of an apostle, evangelist, or pastor.

In the way an apostle is called to lay a foundation in the work of the Lord, the prophet is called to build upon that foundation and work in harmony with the apostle. We understand this more clearly when we bear in mind that the purpose of the gift of prophecy is to edify and exhort and comfort (1 Corinthians 14:3). The function of the prophet is to build and strengthen the congregation of the Lord. The few references we have in Scripture indicate that a prophet is similar to what we call a lay preacher. Prophets are frequently, even regularly, used by the Spirit to prick the conscience of the church. Their work, like the gift of prophecy, serves the believer rather than the unbeliever (1 Corinthians 14:22, 29-31).

Some have come to think of prophets as those who foretell future events; popular understanding of prophecy has narrowed to that single dimension. This has happened because there is indeed an element of foretelling the future in the work of prophecy, and consideration of future events suggests mystery and mysticism that fascinates man. Foretelling the future is but only a small part of a prophet's total work. The root term for "prophet" connotes "one who boils over." A prophet is one who is so filled with Divine anointing that he must proclaim the pent-up Word within him. Jeremiah recorded the circumstances of his call, in the course of which he also gave a resume of the prophetic work, "Then the Lord put forth his hand, and touched my mouth. And the Lord said unto me, Behold, I have put my words in thy mouth. See, I have this day set thee over the nations and over the kingdoms, to root out, and to pull down, and to destroy, and to throw down, to build, and to plant" (Jeremiah 1:9, 10).

Among the New Testament prophets were Silas, who assisted Paul in his missionary work and a man named Judas (Acts 15:32). The work of Silas and Judas consisted largely of consolation and confirmation (vv. 31, 32, 41). Agabus was another prominent prophet of the early church. He with other prophets went from Jerusalem to Antioch, where he foretold an imminent famine (Acts 11:27, 28). On another occasion Agabus foretold the arrest and persecution of Paul (Acts 21:10, 11). The evangelist Philip had four daughters who were prophetesses (Acts 21:8, 9), but we are not told the nature or circumstances of their work.

Whereas the work of apostles was the laying of a foundation, and the work of teachers was orderly and logical instruction, it is clear that the work of prophets was emotional, even ecstatic, exhortation. There is a strong similarity of the work of the Old Testament prophets and the work of John the Baptist, and the prophetic ministry to the early church. It was essentially spontaneous, unpolished, emotional, exhortative, and corrective.

The prophetic ministry is very much in evidence among us today. We do not speak of men as being prophets anymore, but that is exactly what they are when they fulfill the function of a prophet. Much of the Pentecostal ministry is prophetic in nature, exhortative, emotional and urgent, the rooting out of evil and the building up of righteousness. The prophetic ministry in the Pentecostal Revival has always been prominent. The emotional preaching of a prophet may lack the form, the order, and the logic of a teacher or pastor, but it is not to be despised or discarded.

Prophets of Christ relate to the other ministries of the church much as the prophets of the Old Testament related to the priests of that day. Both perform a vital service to the kingdom of God, but they approach the work differently. The Old Testament prophets were not products of the Levitical system; they came from common stock and the most unlikely occupations, such as vinedressers and herdsmen. It has been the same with modern prophets: they have not come from expected sources, but from farms, factories, and the most ordinary backgrounds.

The validity of the prophet's office and service does not in any way justify men in careless habits of study and preparation. The work of the prophet should not become second-rate just because it is rarely formal. Donald Gee gives an excellent warning in this regard:

> A word of warning is required lest this truly God-given gift and ministry should be confused with the lazy, slipshod habits of some preachers who waste precious hours which should be spent in preparation, and then expect the Holy Spirit to help them out by a last-minute revelation. Such often quote, "Open thy mouth wide and I will fill it," but

their messages are usually not such as to bring much glory to
the supposed divine giver. A true prophet does need preparation, as much as any preacher, but it is the preparation
particularly of the heart. He has to "prophesy according to
the proportion of faith" (Romans 12:6), and his faith must
be kept living, strong and enlightened by hours of communion with God.[18]

God's anointing upon His prophets, so that they become
consciences of the church in the same way the prophets of
old became the conscience of Israel, is one of the most
forceful and telling works of the Holy Spirit. The church
should take care that the ministry of prophecy is never
minimized or diminished in its service.

3. EVANGELISTS

The third ministry gift is that of evangelist, which is one
of the most interesting and important of the Gifts. The
word "evangelist" occurs only three times in Scripture, one
being in Paul's listing to the Ephesians, "And he gave some,
. . . evangelists" (Ephesians 4:11). In addition, we read of
"Philip, the evangelist, which was one of the seven" (Acts
21:8), and Timothy, to whom Paul wrote, "watch thou in
all things, endure afflictions, do the work of an evangelist,
make full proof of thy ministry" (2 Timothy 4:5). The
work of evangelism is manifestly one of the most important
works of the Christian ministry, and yet the word "evangelism" is nowhere found in Scripture. The Greek term
from which we get the English word "evangelism" is
euaggelizo, which means "to announce good news." The
word was used by Gabriel when he appeared to Mary with
the news that she would bear a son (Luke 1:19). It also
occurs in the angel's announcement to the shepherds, "I bring
you good tidings of great joy" (Luke 2:10). Paul used the
word *euaggelizo* in Romans 10:15: "And how shall they
preach, except they be sent? as it is written, How beautiful

are the feet of them that preach the gospel of peace, and bring glad tidings of good things!"

An evangelist is one who carries the good tidings of Christ Jesus to those who have not received it. Much like the work of an apostle, although it does not involve the laying of a foundation or require the evangelist to have seen the Lord, the work of evangelism involves taking the news of Christ to the unconverted. Philip, referred to above, did the work of evangelism in Samaria, where the foundation had been laid by Christ Himself when He visited there during His ministry (John 4). The result of Philip's evangelistic preaching was dramatic and joyful, as an entire town turned to the Lord Jesus Christ. In the account of Philip we see real evangelism at work. In the same way, Timothy was admonished to carry the message of Christ to the unconverted, and this young evangelist worked in places where the apostle Paul had laid the foundation.

During New Testament times the apostles and evangelists worked together in reaching men with the gospel. Today the work of evangelism is still a matter of taking the gospel of Christ to the unconverted. The ability and burden to do this is a ministry gift of Christ. Those who are successful evangelists are generally aggressive and forceful; their ministry does not usually involve a great deal of doctrine or instruction, but the persuasive proclamation of salvation in Christ. The great evangelists of the Christian church have often been rough-hewn men, like sharp diamonds cutting deeply into the hard hearts of unregenerate men.

A long-time friend and collegemate of mine, Dr. Ray H. Hughes, who has graced this study with his introduction, is an evangelist of tremendous effectiveness. He and I have worked together in Bible conferences for many years, he the evangelist and I the teacher. I have frequently listened with admiration as he exhorts the unconverted and leads them to Christ, passionately wishing and even praying that I might have such evangelistic effectiveness. I was therefore surprised one day to hear his candid public statement that as he listened to me he often wished for the same ministry in the Word. The ministries of evangelism and teaching have complemented each other from apostolic times to the present.

Evangelism is a prominent and distinguishing feature of the Pentecostal Revival. It is the spearpoint that penetrates every society. When evangelism is slackened the work of God quickly languishes and the kingdom is diminished. Evangelism is God's way of perpetually pressing the frontiers of the kingdom outward.

4. PASTORS

The ministry gift that has continued most prominently from apostolic times to the present is that of the pastor. There seem to be several terms used in the New Testament that refer to pastors, such as "bishops," "elders," and "presbyters," but the term *pastors* has survived through the centuries and is probably the most common term used to designate the ministry today. In this generation the term pastor is almost synonymous with preacher.

The purpose of a pastor is to conserve and consolidate that which has been won to the Lord through evangelism, to strengthen, protect and feed the flock of God. The word "pastor" brings forth all the images of a flock, for the very word means "a shepherd." According to Dr. A. T. Robertson the word *pastor*, "is from a root meaning to protect. Jesus said the good shepherd lays down his life for the sheep (John 10:11) and called Himself the Good Shepherd. In Hebrews 13:20 Christ is the Great Shepherd (cf. 1 Peter 2:25). Only here are preachers termed 'shepherds' (Latin pastors) in the New Testament. But the verb *poimaino,* to shepherd, is employed by Jesus to Peter (John 21:16), by Peter to other ministers (1 Peter 5:2), by Paul to the elders (bishops) of Ephesus (Acts 20:28). Here Paul groups 'shepherds and teachers' together."[19]

In many respects the ministry of the pastor is the most important ministry in the church today. The apostolic foundations have been laid, the work of the prophet is largely exhortative, and the work of the evangelist is dependent upon the pastor. The performance of pastoral work, which is often less dramatic than evangelism or some other function of the ministry, is in many ways the most vital work of all.

Pastor is an Old Testament word, and some of the most telling statements of pastoral responsibility are to be found in the books of Jeremiah and Ezekiel (Jeremiah 2:8; 10: 21; 17:16). The pastor has the spiritual responsibility of a congregation, just as a shepherd has responsibility for his flock. He must lead the flock into good pasture, protect it from all intrusions of danger, and care for those who are weak and lame. The conscientious work of pastors leads to growth in the flock, for the sheep reproduce and bring forth lambs. "And I will give you pastors according to mine heart, which shall feed you with knowledge and understanding" (Jeremiah 3:15).

No one in the New Testament was specifically referred to as a pastor, but there are numerous references to those who were used in this ministry. Through most of the New Testament period there had been no formal break between Judaism and Christianity, and most of the Christians were believers in Christ who still attended the Jewish synagogue. There were nevertheless persons such as Ananias in Damascus who fulfilled the pastor's function. In time, when there would be Christian congregations separate from the Jewish synagogues, the work of pastors would become more prominent and clearly defined. The pastor became responsible to provide his congregation with (1) spiritual leadership, (2) food from the Word of God, (3) protection from danger, and (4) comfort in its afflictions.

Spiritual Leadership. The picture of a pastor and his congregation is precisely the picture of a shepherd and his flock. In fact, the words *shepherd* and *pastor* are the very same, as are the words *flock* and *congregation*. The Lord has used the same imagery to describe the work of this ministry. A pastor must provide his people with the leadership of his example, his courage and his wisdom. He must lead the people to spiritual fullness and enrichment. Evangelistic opportunities occur to the pastor constantly, for it is his responsibility to lead to Christ the unconverted who attend his church. The pastor more than any other ministry will have a combination of all five of the Ministry Gifts. At times each of them will express itself through his activity.

Food from the Word. A career preacher may be tempted to feed his people with light and frivolous preaching just because it is popular, but God's pastor will feel a responsibility to preach the Word in its fullness. He should be so sensitive to God's will and the needs of the people that he will provide them the meat of the Word whereby they can grow (Hebrews 5:12-14). This necessity of spiritual provision becomes the pastor's foremost responsibility, because it is the Word that cleanses, purifies, strengthens and gives growth to those who hear.

Protection from Danger. A pastor is responsible to secure his congregation from the intrusions of heresy and false teaching, which constantly prey upon the people of God. He is a foolish pastor who allows unconfirmed pretenders to enter his pulpit. He should heed the example of the ancient shepherd and his flock: at night the shepherd gathered his sheep into the fold and then slept at the door. Any wolf that entered had to cross over the shepherd's body and any sheep that left had to do the same. This is a graphic example of how a pastor should feel the responsibility to protect his people.

Comfort for Afflictions. As a shepherd was responsible to care for the cuts and bruises and broken limbs of the flock, so the pastor must be skilled in comforting the brokenhearted, encouraging the disspirited and soothing the offended. Jesus was certainly speaking of a pastoral function on the occasion when He read from the prophet Isaiah: "The Spirit of the Lord is upon me, because he hath anointed me to preach the gospel to the poor; he hath sent me to heal the brokenhearted, to preach deliverance to the captives, and recovering of sight to the blind, to set at liberty them that are bruised, To preach the acceptable year of the Lord" (Luke 4:18-19). This is the work of a pastor, which in many ways is the most rewarding work of God's kingdom. A pastor is able to see the young grow to maturity, the weak become strong, the congregation increase. A man with a pastor's heart will carry a constant burden but will day by day find cause for rejoicing.

5. *TEACHERS*

The ministry of teaching is closely related to pastors and is in reality a part of the pastor's function. In Paul's list of the Ministry Gifts, "pastors and teachers" are actually listed together, and the two are generally regarded as one ministry gift. This may be true, I make no argument about that, for both are definitely important to the ministry of watchcare; but I list teaching separately here for the purpose of emphasizing its importance to the

church. Every minister who is called of God must show
some ability in all ministerial manifestations. For instance,
I am sure that there were times when Paul filled the role
of prophet, evangelist, pastor and teacher, as well as that
of apostle. The very same is true today: the pastor is at
times prophet, evangelist and teacher. It is almost impossible to make a precise separation of the Ministry Gifts
and their individual manifestations.

Teaching is important in every expression of the ministry,
for instruction in faith is necessary to the entire kingdom
work. For example, Jesus instructed the apostles to, "go
ye therefore, and teach all nations" (Matthew 28:19). It
is said more often that Jesus taught the people than that
He preached to them (Mark 1:22).

The ministry of teaching was prevalent in the days of
the apostles; so much so that Paul said to the Corinthians,
"Though ye have ten thousand instructers in Christ, yet
have ye not many fathers" (1 Corinthians 4:15). The
number ten thousand was not intended to be literal, for
Paul was simply reminding the Corinthians that many ministers might teach them, but only he had won them to the
Lord. Numerous pastors and teachers are necessary to care
for the souls brought into the kingdom by apostles and
evangelists. The fact that the ministry of teaching is listed
alone in 1 Corinthians 12:29 places emphasis on the importance of teaching even as a part of the pastoral role.

ROLE OF THE MIND

Christian teaching is of highest importance to the work
of Christ. It can be defined as a systematic process of
reasoning and instruction whereby the truths of God are
established in the hearts of the hearers. Effective teaching
is deliberate but enthusiastic, well-reasoned but earnest. It
is aimed more at the intellect and reasoning ability of

men than to the feelings and emotions. All preaching
should involve the intellectual processes of man.

Frequently in the early days of the Pentecostal Movement
a person might hear such statements as, "Religion is of the
heart and not of the mind." This was a foolish and incorrect
expression. Although the purpose was to point up the need
of heartfelt commitment to Christ, the result of such think-
ing was injurious to the church. Religion is definitely a
matter of the mind. The word "conviction," used to speak
of a person's awareness of his need of salvation, means a
change of mind. When a man is convinced of his need of
Christ he is "under conviction."

Christians overcome the world by a renewing of the mind
(Romans 12:2); are instructed to arm themselves with the
same mind that was in Christ Jesus (1 Peter 4:1); are told to
gird up the loins of their minds (1 Peter 1:13); and to stir
up their pure minds (2 Peter 3:1). Paul tells men to let the
mind of Christ be in them (Philippians 2:5); and the
Lord gives men the spirit of a sound mind (2 Timothy 1:7).

The Scriptures are virtually permeated with references to
the role of the mind in spiritual living. It is essential that
the Christian mind be instructed, fortified, set and determined in the way of Christ. It is not enough to pray until
we have good feelings and then trust ourselves thereafter
to those feelings. Our mind must be overwhelmed with the
truth of Christ; it must be involved and committed in the
life of holiness and righteousness.

Much attention was given to teaching in the early days
of the Pentecostal Movement. This ministry is no less
important to us today. Alongside the strong emotional
quality of the Revival, much emphasis was placed on teaching, and many of the great giants of the Movement exercised a ministry of teaching. This care of instruction,

coupled with enthusiastic evangelism, is responsible for the growth and maturity of the Movement.

As it is with the Gifts of the Spirit, some Ministry Gifts are less spectacular than others, but no less important. Teaching may be less dramatic than evangelism, less emotional than prophecy, but it is no less important. It is quite likely that greater emphasis is placed on teaching in the Scriptures than any other ministry gift. Certainly it is mentioned more often. We have a great responsibility in this regard, for teaching is the ministry by which the church is made solid and enduring.

6. ADMINISTRATION

Let me repeat that the threefold purpose of the ministry is (1) evangelism, (2) watchcare, and (3) administration. Strangely, there are some today who accept without hesitation the ministries of evangelism and watchcare, but reject church administration. This is unfortunate, for the exercise of government in the church is as spiritual and as necessary as any other ministry. According to Peter, the despising of government, and that means church government, is a sign of the apostasy of the last days (2 Peter 2:10). The purpose of church administration is to provide order, unity, direction, and regulation to the work of Christ. The word "governments," used by Paul in 1 Corinthians 12:28, comes from the Greek word *kubernao* which means "to administer or govern."

Government is a blessing and gift of God. From the beginning of time steam has been produced by fire and water, but the steam did not benefit man until it was harnessed. When it is brought under control and given purpose it is able to propel ships across the seas, drive trains with heavy cargo across the land, turn motors and machinery that operate plants and factories, and do other beneficial works. Electricity is the same. When it flashes without control in the form of lightning, it can be destructive and fatal. Harness it, however, and it lights large cities, furnishes heat in winter, cold in summer, and serves man in innumerable ways. For years the Tennessee River flooded frequently and brought widespread destruction and loss to the Tennessee Valley. During the 1930s the river was brought under control by a series of dams that eliminated the flooding and produced electrical power for the region. By harnessing the wild river it has become a benefactor and a blessing.

God has not given church government in order to inhibit or retard His work, but to give it order and purpose, coordination and effectiveness. In scripture church government is likened to the functions of the human body (1 Corinthians 12:12-26). The primary purpose of this analogy is to show the necessity for and cooperation of the various ministries of the church. A secondary effect of the analogy is to show how each part of the human body is under the government or administration of the head. The feet do not walk and the hands do not work by their own will, but they do what the head directs them to do. Our bodily parts cannot work at variance with one another, for they are given unified direction by the mind. Without this administration the feet, the hands, the eyes, the ears, the nose and the head would work independent of one another so that the result would become disorder, frustration and confusion.

The ministry of Paul is a splendid example of Divine government in operation. As an administrator he assigned men to various responsibilities. Read 2 Timothy 4:9-12 and Titus 1:5; 3:12, and you will see that he (1) sent for Timothy, (2) sent for Mark, (3) sent Tychicus to Ephesus, and (4) left Trophimus in Miletus, (5) assigned Titus to

Crete, (6) appointed Titus an elder, (7) and sent Artemus or Tychicus to Titus. After freely assigning men to particular tasks, Paul was quite willing to submit himself in turn to those who had the rule over him. The fifteenth chapter of Acts gives an account of his submission to the judgment of the church leadership regarding circumcision. An equally dramatic instance is when Paul submitted himself to James and the elders of the church in Acts 21:18-26. They directed Paul to join himself to four brethren and perform certain Jewish rituals in order to dispel the rumor that he had turned against his people. Paul did not resent the instruction but followed the counsel of James and the elders.

God has not called church administrators to be overlords and church dictators, but to be humble and meek servants of the Lord Jesus Christ. When the ministry works together with the acceptance of God's plan for order, then the work of the church will be harmonious and powerful. It is when we become out of joint or out of balance that we begin to have problems. The ministry is given to be a blessing, a benefit, a gift in the work of the Lord.

SUMMARY

Christ came to earth to bring the kingdom of God to men. An inescapable consequence of His incarnation was that His earthly life must end in death. He could not be totally incarnate and live on earth forever. His incarnation therefore imposed the necessity of extending His life and ministry in another way. This extension of Himself is in the form of the church, chosen men and women who continue in their lives and by their works to show Him to their generation. He is the Head and we are His body. Everything we do must be done at His word and in accordance with His will.

The question we should ask ourselves, then, is what would
Jesus do if He were still alive on earth? What He would
do, we must do. Such a responsibility is far too great for
mortal man and natural strength. Christ has therefore
given His church three elements that produce the fruit of
His life, just as a branch produces the fruit of the vine.
These elements are the Fruit of the Spirit, Gifts of the
Spirit and the Ministry Gifts. They are of separate function and yet they work together in the performance of the
church. They are balanced, harmonious and unified, absolutely essential for us to be His continuing representatives
on earth. This has been God's plan from the beginning
and it shall always be.

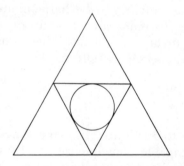

APPENDICES

REFERENCES

[1]Augustus Hopkins Strong, *Systematic Theology* (Philadelphia: Judson Press, 1907), p. 304.

[2]Lewis Sperry Chafer, *Major Bible Themes* (Wheaton: Van Kampen Press, 1926), p. 21.

[3]R. A. Torrey, *What The Bible Teaches* (New York: Fleming H. Revell, 1933), p. 99.

[4]J. B. Phillips, *New Testament Christianity* (London: Hodder and Stoughton Ltd., 1958), pp. 120-121.

[5]Stephen Neill, *The Christian Character* (London: Lutterworth Press, 1955), p. 41.

[6]W. L. Walker, "Goodness," *The International Standard Bible Encyclopedia* (Grand Rapids: William B. Eerdmans Publishing Company, 1939), Vol. 2, p. 1279.

[7]Andrew Murray, *Humility* (New York: Fleming H. Revell Company, n. d.), pp. 12 ff.

[8]Quoted in Frank S. Mead, *Encyclopedia of Religious Quotations* (Westwood, N. J.: Fleming H. Revell Company, 1965), p. 238.

[9]*Ibid.*, p. 237.

[10]Murray, *op. cit.*, p. 52 f.

[11]*The Works of John Wesley* (Grand Rapids: Zondervan Publishing House, Reprint edition of 1872), Vol. 5, p. 353.

[12]Arthur Wallis, *God's Chosen Fast* (Ft. Washington, Pa.: Christian Literature Crusade, 1968), p. 10.

[13]R. E. McAlister, *The Manifestations of the Spirit* (Toronto: Full Gospel Publishing House, n. d.), p. 13.

[14]*Ibid.*, p. 3 f.

[15]Donald Gee, *Concerning Spiritual Gifts* (Springfield, Missouri: Gospel Publishing House, 1928), p. 30.

[16]Harold Horton, *The Gifts of the Spirit* (London: Assemblies of God Publishing House, 1930), p. 41.

[17]Donald Gee, *The Ministry-Gifts of Christ* (Springfield, Missouri: Gospel Publishing House, 1930), p. 14.

[18]*Ibid.*, 41.

[19]Archibald Thomas Robertson, *Word Pictures in the New Testament* (New York: Harper & Row Publishers, 1931), Vol. 4, p. 537.

INDEX TO SCRIPTURAL REFERENCES

o

GENERAL INDEX

Abraham, 69
Achan, 122
Adam, 26
Administrators, (see Ministry Gifts)
Agabus, 116, 133, 155
Agrippa, King, 147
Ai, 122
Ananias, 87, 116, 160
Andrew, 146
Andronicus, 153
Anna, 94
Anxiety, 49
Apostasy, dangers of, 30, 31, 108, 161
Apostles, (see Ministry Gifts)
Artimus, 166
Automobiles, illustration of, 109

Barnabas, 73, 75, 76, 147, 153
Beasts, nature of, 27
Bishops, (see Ministry Gifts)
Brooks, Philips (quoted), 83

Cana of Galilee, 130
Chafer, Lewis Sperry (quoted), 24
"Charismatic Renewal," the, 101
Christ, see Jesus Christ
Conn, Edna Minor, 124-125, 127-128, 139
Conscience, 27, 28
Cornelius, 116, 136
Courage, 49, 51

Damascus, 116
Daniel, 94
Deacons, (see Ministry Gifts)
Demons, and demon-possession, 118-120, 121, 129, 130, 131
Discerning of spirits, (see Gifts of the Spirit)
Dorcas, 76, 131

Edwards, Tryon (quoted), 83
Elders, (see Ministry Gifts)
Elijah, 94
Elymas, 87, 121
Emotions, human, 47-51
  expressions of, 48-50, 155, 156
Ephesus, 136
Esau, 92
Eternity, 27, 28
Evangelists, (see Ministry Gifts)
Eutychus, 131
Eve, 26

Faith, (see Fruit of the Spirit)
  (see Gifts of the Spirit)
Fanaticism, danger of, 30, 35, 37, 108, 109, 150, 161
Fasting, 93-94, 124-125, 128, 130
Fear, 49, 51
Fellowship, Christian, 65, 66, 67
  threefold, 28
Fruit of the Spirit, 30-33, 41-46, 99, 100, 102, 103, 123, 136, 142, 151, 168
  love, 47, 48, 51-56
  joy 48, 56-61
  peace, 49, 61-66
  longsuffering (patience), 68-71
  gentleness (kindness), 71-73
  goodness, 74-77
  faith (faithfulness), 77, 78-81
  meekness (humility), 81-88
  temperance (self-control), 89-94

Gabriel, 157
Gadarenes, the, 147
Gee, Donald (quoted), 115, 148, 156-157
Gentleness (see Fruit of the Spirit)
Gifts of the Spirit, 30, 33-35, 36, 37, 99-112
  wisdom, word of, 112, 113-115
  knowledge, word of, 112, 115-118
  discerning of spirits, 112, 118-122
  faith, 80, 112, 123-126
  healings, gifts of, 101, 107, 112, 122, 123-125, 126-129, 131
  miracles, 112, 129-132
  prophecy, 112, 133-135, 138
  tongues, 112, 135-140, 141
  interpretation of tongues, 112, 140-142
Godhead, (see Trinity)
Goodness, (see Fruit of the Spirit)
Government, Divine, 150, 165-167

Hannah, 94
Happiness, 57-58, 59, 60
Hate, 47
Healing, gifts of, (see Gifts of the Spirit)
  instances of, 123-125, 127-129
Holiness, 29, 42, 43, 84, 85, 86, 88, 145, 164
Holy Spirit, the, 19, 43, 44, 89, 91-92, 103-104, 119, 120, 132, 133, 142
  promised by Jesus 16, 19, 99

source of the Spirit, 43-44
work of regeneration, 44, 100
enemy of the flesh, 78, 91, 92
Baptism of, 44, 78, 100, 101, 108, 127, 132, 136, 137, 138
and the emotions, 48-51
Hong Kong, 120
Horton, Harold (quoted), 129
Hughes, Ray H., 158

Interpretation of Tongues, (see Gifts of the Spirit)
Israelites, 69

James, 167
Jeremiah, 155
Jericho, 122
Jesus Christ, 15-17, 30, 32, 33, 45, 56, 61, 63, 66, 94, 99, 114, 142, 152, 158, 162, 167
and the church, 17-18, 23, 30, 41, 65, 99, 100, 114, 142, 145, 148, 158, 167
limitations of Incarnation, 17, 167, 103
illustrations of fruitfulness, 31-32
the Son of God, 43
atonement by, 45
His holiness, 43
and love, 51-54, 55
and joy, 57, 59, 61
birth, 61, 69
His peace, 61-62
Second coming, 63
His Crucifixion, 61, 75, 76, 88, 104
His meekness, 86-87, 88
His miracles, 109-110, 130
and the Rich Young Ruler, 74
a good man, 75
calls men to discipleship, 146-147
an apostle, 152
Job, 81
John the Baptist, 155
Joseph of Arimathea, 75
Joy, (see Fruit of the Spirit)
Judas, 155
Judas Iscariot, 152
Junia, 153

Knowledge, word of, (see Gifts of the Spirit)
Korea,

Lee College, 139
"Legion," 147
Longsuffering, (see Fruit of the Spirit)

Love, (see Fruit of the Spirit)

Man:
the image of God, 25-28
his will, 27
his conscience, 28
eternal, 28
communion with God, 28-30
his Christlikeness, 41-43, 44, 46, 48
responsibility for purity, 45-46
his emotions, 48-51
fellowship with others, 62-64, 66-67, 84
his selfishness, 64, 78
his patience, 69-70
meaning of "gentleman," 72
wishes to be good, 74
his humility, 84-86
his body, 90-91
his mind, 94, 163-164
temple of the Holy Spirit, 91-92
used to reach other men, 145-149
Mark, 73, 166
Matthew, 146
Matthias, 153
McAlister, R. E. (quoted), 106, 114
Meekness, (see Fruit of the Spirit)
Mind, the human, 163-164
Ministry Gifts, the, 35-37, 133, 145-151, 164, 168
apostles, 147, 151, 152-154
prophets, 133, 151, 154-157
evangelists, 149, 150, 151, 157-159, 160
pastors, 149, 150, 151, 159-162
teachers, 149, 150, 151, 162-165
administrators, 149, 150, 165-167
bishops, 151, 159, 160
deacons, 151
presbyters, 151, 159, 160
elders, 159, 160
Miracles, (see Gifts of the Spirit)
Missouri, 127
Moses, 69, 70, 87, 88, 89
Murray, Andrew (quoted), 82, 85

Nathaniel, 146
Neill, Stephen (quoted), 65, 74

Pastors, (see Ministry Gifts)
Paul, the apostle:
his writings, 65
example of longsuffering, 68-69
his meekness, 87, 88

COMMENTS

EARLIER BOOKS BY Dr. Charles W. Conn have been the result of months and years of research. This present volume, *A Balanced Church*, is similarly and unmistakably the result of much research in the Scriptures and a lifetime of scholastic and pastoral ministry.

Dr. Conn gives a beautiful scriptural description of the Trinity. He ably expounds the freewill of man in simple language and easy to be understood, and submits with great clarity, "The Fruit of the Spirit," "The Gifts of the Spirit," and "The Ministry Gifts of Christ."

I like the term, "The Church is the extension of Christ," for in it Jesus Christ and His commission are given their rightful place in the life of the modern church. In establishing His church our Lord left nothing to chance. A "balanced church" is one with a correct understanding and appropriation of the Fruit of the Spirit, the Gifts of the Spirit and the Ministry Gifts.

I would certainly like to see every Pentecostal minister read this treatise on the Fruit, the Gifts and the Ministry. It is timely and appropriate that a book of this nature should come from the pen of a man such as Charles W. Conn. The Pentecostal people are the champions of truth and especially the sacred truth concerning Christ's church. And Dr. Conn has a profound relationship with and understanding of the Pentecostal experience.

It is perhaps unusual that the president of a large and influential college should major on the subject of "A Balanced Church," but few men could have been better qualified to write on the subject. The whole spiritual tenor of the book reflects the personality of the author. Dr. Conn takes great interest in World Pentecostal Conferences and has held positions on its highest council, the Advisory Committee, He has also served with outstanding distinction of the General Overseer of his Movement. To know Dr. Conn and to visit Lee College, where he is the president, immediately creates a desire to read his books. He is a thorough scholar, an ardent minister, a devoted father, and a spiritual man. The British people testified when he preached in the British Isles that he was a man of God and an outstanding preacher of truth.

I like the title, "A Balanced Church." Balance is the ideal and should be the goal of every local assembly. There is a dearth of sane books on church life, and this book should prove to be a balance to some who are caught up in the trap of loose, or non-church loyalty. The doctrines are brought to life, the words of Jesus and His disciples are stimulating. Indeed the lack of balance and wisdom has caused havoc among some churches and Movements. I, therefore, heartily commend this book and know it will serve the church well in this generation.

PERCY S. BREWSTER
Secretary-General,
Elim Pentecostal Churches
Secretary,
Pentecostal World Conference

ANOTHER SOUND SCRIPTURAL book is on its way into pastors' studies and libraries. It comes from the pen of a prolific writer, the Reverend Dr. Charles W. Conn, whose gifts and qualities in this field are unquestionable. He is widely recognized as a great religious writer of our day. He has authored many books, including *Pillars of Pentecost, Where the Saints Have Trod, Acts of the Apostles* and *Christ and the Gospels.*

Dr. Conn has the unusual ability of making great truths plain and practical. This is the uniqueness of his writing. His qualities come to light in transforming the seemingly small and insignificant into the great and invaluable. This book, *A Balanced Church,* is no exception. It deserves to be read, and it will be. And I predict that many ministers and laymen alike will be blessed by its contents.

May God's richest blessings accompany it on its mission of enlightenment and inspiration.

WADE H. HORTON
General Overseer
Church of God

I APPRECIATE THIS BOOK on *A Balanced Church* for its time-
liness. It speaks to those proven and time-worn issues which are being
reassessed in our day by a host of Charismatic oncomers. Never have I
leaped so immediately into the rich content of a book. I was so
inspired that I had to pause to meditate on the very first page.

> *RAY E. SMITH*
> *General Superintendent*
> *Open Bible Standard Churches, Inc.*

A BALANCED CHURCH is a stimulating and inspiring book, an
outstanding contribution to the church in these challenging days when
scriptural balance is of such overriding, vital and critical importance.
I have been edified and instructed as I have read it prayerfully.

In my estimation the author himself is one imminently qualified
as a man of great talents, spirituality and balance in all phases of his
life and ministry.

I look forward to seeing the book in its published form.

> *HOWARD P. COURTNEY*
> *Vice-President*
> *International Church of the Foursquare Gospel*

IN HIS NEWEST BOOK, *A Balanced Church,* Dr. Charles W. Conn
has shown the ability to set forth Pentecostal doctrine in a uniquely
practical approach. Building this splendid teaching source on a
foundation of triads he has related the teaching of the Trinity,
the church, the Fruit of the Spirit, Gifts of the Spirit, and Ministry
Gifts of the Spirit in an unusual manner. His treatment of demon-
ism, healing and other currently debated topics is thought-provoking
and incisive. It will prove to be an excellent reference and teaching
source, comprehensive in scope and inspirational in its presentation.

> *ROBERT W. TAITINGER*
> *General Superintendent*
> *The Pentecostal Assemblies of Canada*

IT WAS MY PRIVILEGE to hear the lectures that were delivered by Dr. Charles W. Conn as they were presented during the King Memorial Lecture Series in Franklin Springs, Georgia. I thrilled to the expertise that was clearly in evidence as he "rightly divided the word of truth." With beautiful simplicity he explained some of the deep and mysterious theological truths of the Bible.

The volume he has prepared is well written and will serve to instruct and inspire the serious searchers for exquisite and precious truths.

J. FLOYD WILLIAMS
General Superintendent
Pentecostal Holiness Church

DR. CHARLES W. CONN has performed a great service in providing a book which shows the need of balance in relation to the Fruit of the Spirit, the Gifts of the Spirit, and the Ministry Gifts of Christ. In his thorough exposition of this important area of truth, the author has not hesitated to carefully and kindly consider problems and errors which have recently arisen in some Pentecostal circles. From his own rich ministerial background and frame of reference he deals forthrightly and clearly with many controversial areas. Bible students will find this timely volume to be a source of inspirational reading, a ready reference work, or a textbook for classes.

THOMAS F. ZIMMERMAN
General Superintendent
Assemblies of God
Chairman, Advisory Committee
Pentecostal World Conference